AN EXCHANGE OF GIFTS

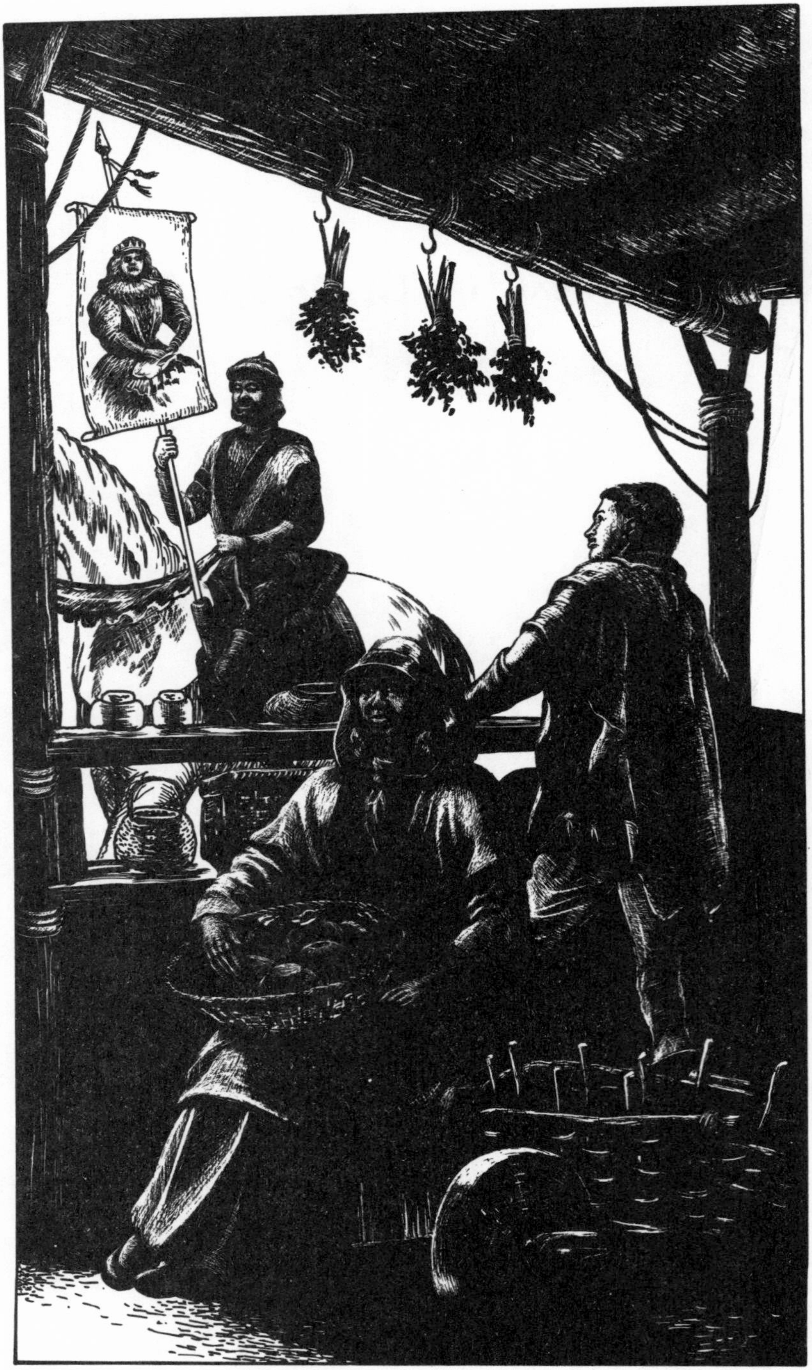

AN EXCHANGE OF GIFTS

by Anne McCaffrey

Illustrated by

Pat Morrissey

The Wildside Press
Newark, NJ 1995

AN EXCHANGE OF GIFTS

The Wildside Press
37 Fillmore Street
Newark, NJ 07105.

ISBN: 1-880448-48-3

To Ceara Rose McCaffrey—
a little tale for a little granddaughter that
she may enjoy more when she's a tad older.

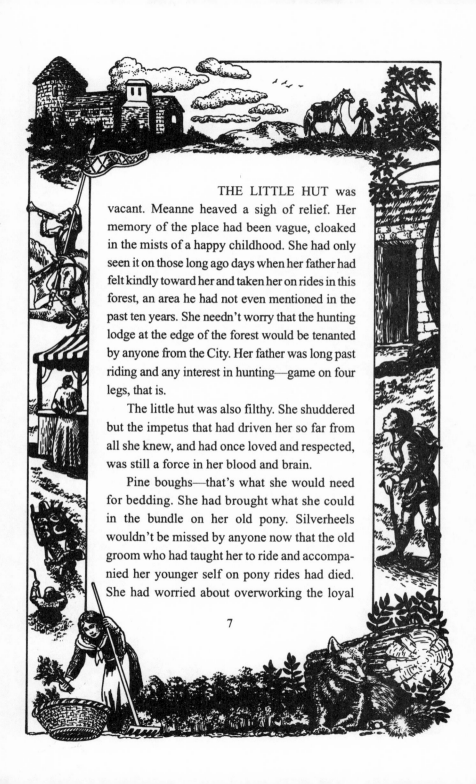

THE LITTLE HUT was vacant. Meanne heaved a sigh of relief. Her memory of the place had been vague, cloaked in the mists of a happy childhood. She had only seen it on those long ago days when her father had felt kindly toward her and taken her on rides in this forest, an area he had not even mentioned in the past ten years. She needn't worry that the hunting lodge at the edge of the forest would be tenanted by anyone from the City. Her father was long past riding and any interest in hunting—game on four legs, that is.

The little hut was also filthy. She shuddered but the impetus that had driven her so far from all she knew, and had once loved and respected, was still a force in her blood and brain.

Pine boughs—that's what she would need for bedding. She had brought what she could in the bundle on her old pony. Silverheels wouldn't be missed by anyone now that the old groom who had taught her to ride and accompanied her younger self on pony rides had died. She had worried about overworking the loyal

7

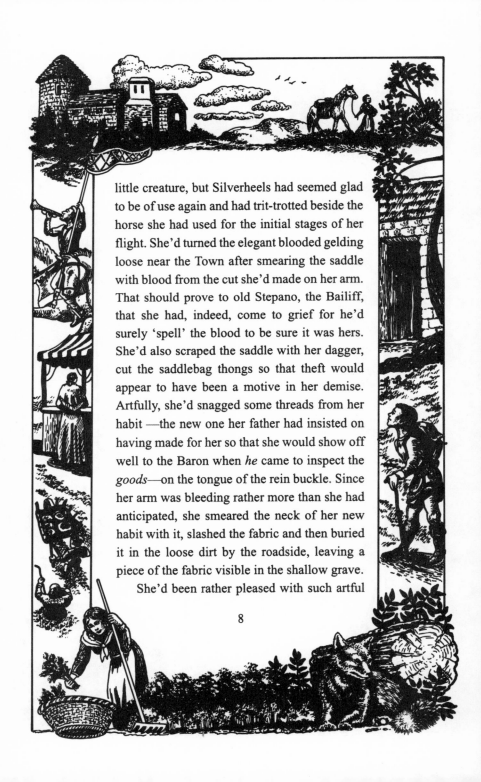

little creature, but Silverheels had seemed glad to be of use again and had trit-trotted beside the horse she had used for the initial stages of her flight. She'd turned the elegant blooded gelding loose near the Town after smearing the saddle with blood from the cut she'd made on her arm. That should prove to old Stepano, the Bailiff, that she had, indeed, come to grief for he'd surely 'spell' the blood to be sure it was hers. She'd also scraped the saddle with her dagger, cut the saddlebag thongs so that theft would appear to have been a motive in her demise. Artfully, she'd snagged some threads from her habit —the new one her father had insisted on having made for her so that she would show off well to the Baron when *he* came to inspect the *goods*—on the tongue of the rein buckle. Since her arm was bleeding rather more than she had anticipated, she smeared the neck of her new habit with it, slashed the fabric and then buried it in the loose dirt by the roadside, leaving a piece of the fabric visible in the shallow grave.

She'd been rather pleased with such artful

8

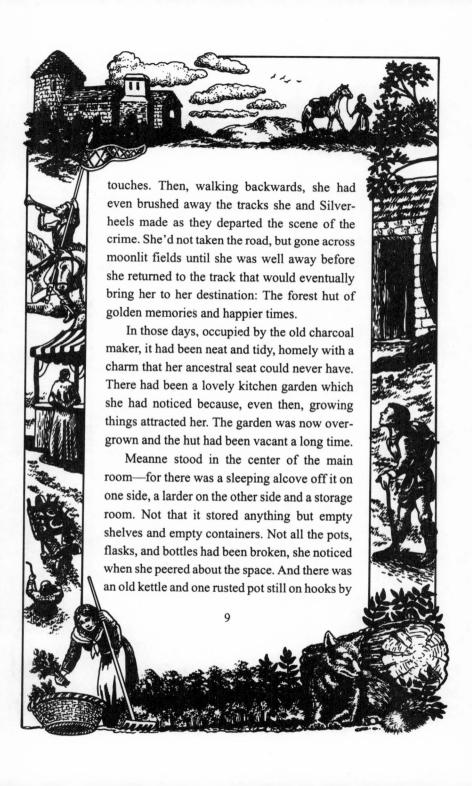

touches. Then, walking backwards, she had even brushed away the tracks she and Silverheels made as they departed the scene of the crime. She'd not taken the road, but gone across moonlit fields until she was well away before she returned to the track that would eventually bring her to her destination: The forest hut of golden memories and happier times.

In those days, occupied by the old charcoal maker, it had been neat and tidy, homely with a charm that her ancestral seat could never have. There had been a lovely kitchen garden which she had noticed because, even then, growing things attracted her. The garden was now overgrown and the hut had been vacant a long time.

Meanne stood in the center of the main room—for there was a sleeping alcove off it on one side, a larder on the other side and a storage room. Not that it stored anything but empty shelves and empty containers. Not all the pots, flasks, and bottles had been broken, she noticed when she peered about the space. And there was an old kettle and one rusted pot still on hooks by

9

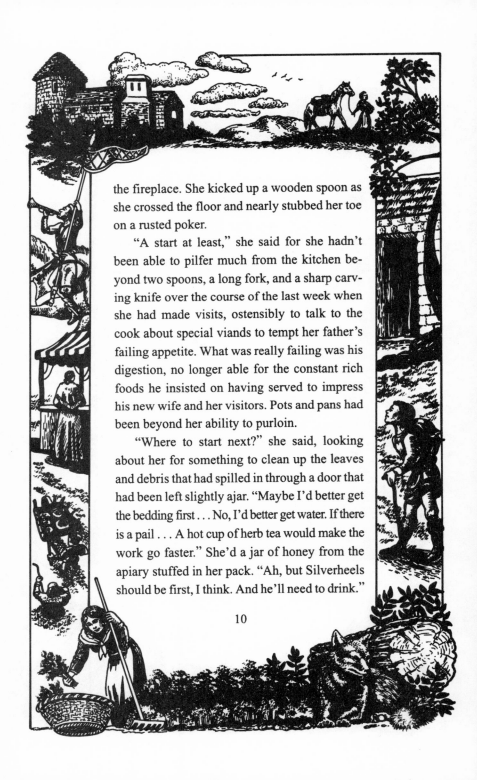

the fireplace. She kicked up a wooden spoon as she crossed the floor and nearly stubbed her toe on a rusted poker.

"A start at least," she said for she hadn't been able to pilfer much from the kitchen beyond two spoons, a long fork, and a sharp carving knife over the course of the last week when she had made visits, ostensibly to talk to the cook about special viands to tempt her father's failing appetite. What was really failing was his digestion, no longer able for the constant rich foods he insisted on having served to impress his new wife and her visitors. Pots and pans had been beyond her ability to purloin.

"Where to start next?" she said, looking about her for something to clean up the leaves and debris that had spilled in through a door that had been left slightly ajar. "Maybe I'd better get the bedding first . . . No, I'd better get water. If there is a pail . . . A hot cup of herb tea would make the work go faster." She'd a jar of honey from the apiary stuffed in her pack. "Ah, but Silverheels should be first, I think. And he'll need to drink."

10

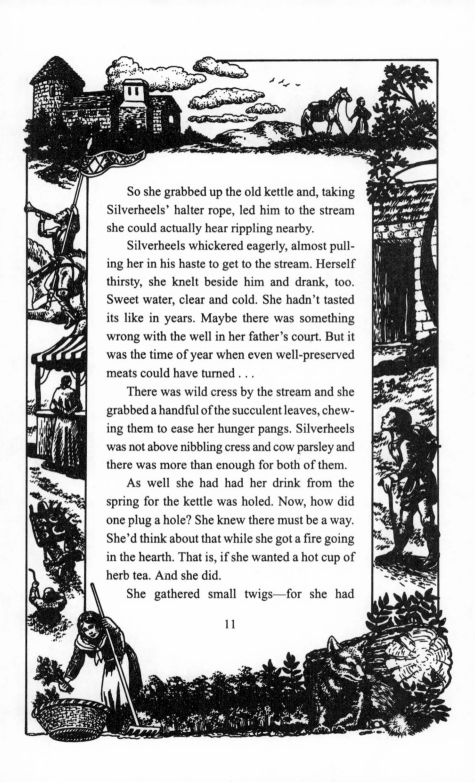

So she grabbed up the old kettle and, taking Silverheels' halter rope, led him to the stream she could actually hear rippling nearby.

Silverheels whickered eagerly, almost pulling her in his haste to get to the stream. Herself thirsty, she knelt beside him and drank, too. Sweet water, clear and cold. She hadn't tasted its like in years. Maybe there was something wrong with the well in her father's court. But it was the time of year when even well-preserved meats could have turned . . .

There was wild cress by the stream and she grabbed a handful of the succulent leaves, chewing them to ease her hunger pangs. Silverheels was not above nibbling cress and cow parsley and there was more than enough for both of them.

As well she had had her drink from the spring for the kettle was holed. Now, how did one plug a hole? She knew there must be a way. She'd think about that while she got a fire going in the hearth. That is, if she wanted a hot cup of herb tea. And she did.

She gathered small twigs—for she had

11

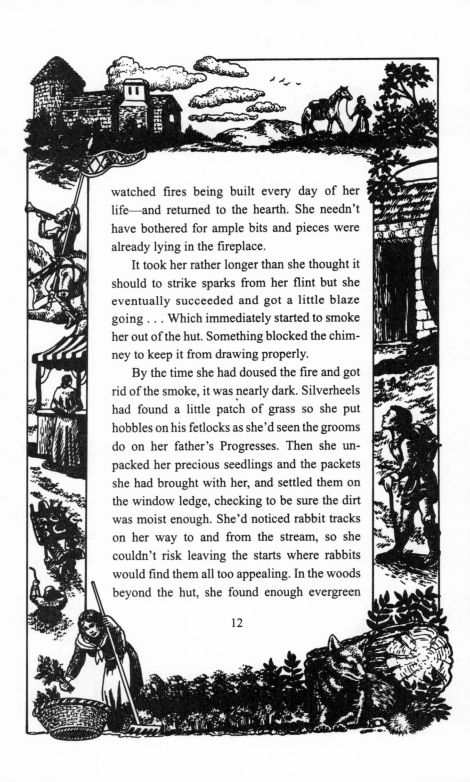

watched fires being built every day of her life—and returned to the hearth. She needn't have bothered for ample bits and pieces were already lying in the fireplace.

It took her rather longer than she thought it should to strike sparks from her flint but she eventually succeeded and got a little blaze going . . . Which immediately started to smoke her out of the hut. Something blocked the chimney to keep it from drawing properly.

By the time she had doused the fire and got rid of the smoke, it was nearly dark. Silverheels had found a little patch of grass so she put hobbles on his fetlocks as she'd seen the grooms do on her father's Progresses. Then she unpacked her precious seedlings and the packets she had brought with her, and settled them on the window ledge, checking to be sure the dirt was moist enough. She'd noticed rabbit tracks on her way to and from the stream, so she couldn't risk leaving the starts where rabbits would find them all too appealing. In the woods beyond the hut, she found enough evergreen

12

boughs to cushion her bones from the hard-packed ground . . . because the slats of the bed were missing . . . and by spreading her cloak and all the clothing she'd brought with her, she managed to get herself comfortable enough to sleep.

She did get to sleep—just before dawn—having had to argue herself out of fear because of all the night noises she had not expected to have to identify. Squeakings and scratchings, odd clicks and soft thuds and wind noises which sounded more threatening, and hootings and an amazing vocabulary of sounds that kept her from the repose she so earnestly sought.

She ached when she finally conceded defeat on the matter of sleep. By the time night had fallen her second night in the hut, she had about conceded defeat on every attempt she had initiated to establish herself suitably and with a modicum of comfort in the hut. It had *seemed* such a good idea—living by herself without having to consult half a dozen people to gain

13

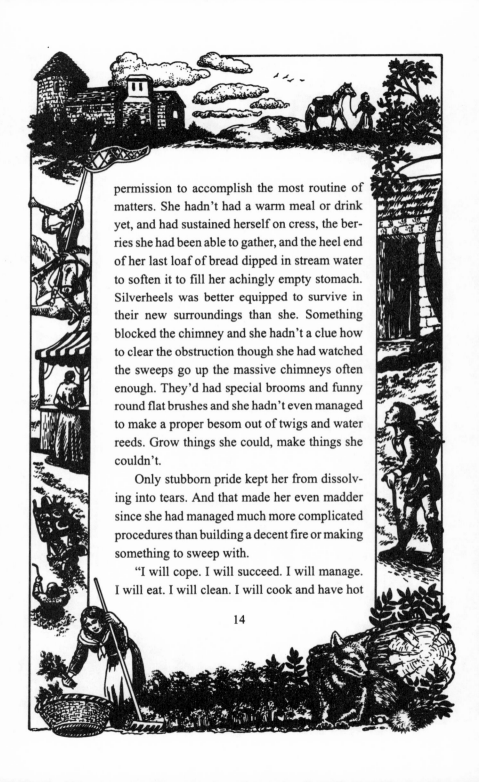

permission to accomplish the most routine of matters. She hadn't had a warm meal or drink yet, and had sustained herself on cress, the berries she had been able to gather, and the heel end of her last loaf of bread dipped in stream water to soften it to fill her achingly empty stomach. Silverheels was better equipped to survive in their new surroundings than she. Something blocked the chimney and she hadn't a clue how to clear the obstruction though she had watched the sweeps go up the massive chimneys often enough. They'd had special brooms and funny round flat brushes and she hadn't even managed to make a proper besom out of twigs and water reeds. Grow things she could, make things she couldn't.

Only stubborn pride kept her from dissolving into tears. And that made her even madder since she had managed much more complicated procedures than building a decent fire or making something to sweep with.

"I will cope. I will succeed. I will manage. I will eat. I will clean. I will cook and have hot

14

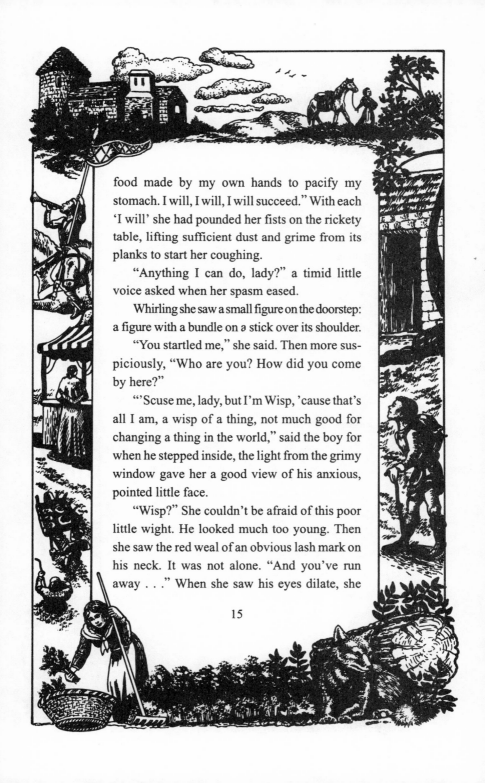

food made by my own hands to pacify my stomach. I will, I will, I will succeed." With each 'I will' she had pounded her fists on the rickety table, lifting sufficient dust and grime from its planks to start her coughing.

"Anything I can do, lady?" a timid little voice asked when her spasm eased.

Whirling she saw a small figure on the doorstep: a figure with a bundle on a stick over its shoulder.

"You startled me," she said. Then more suspiciously, "Who are you? How did you come by here?"

"'Scuse me, lady, but I'm Wisp, 'cause that's all I am, a wisp of a thing, not much good for changing a thing in the world," said the boy for when he stepped inside, the light from the grimy window gave her a good view of his anxious, pointed little face.

"Wisp?" She couldn't be afraid of this poor little wight. He looked much too young. Then she saw the red weal of an obvious lash mark on his neck. It was not alone. "And you've run away . . ." When she saw his eyes dilate, she

15

added, with a wry grin, "like me?"

He relaxed for he'd looked about to run back into the failing light.

"Yes, lady." His answering grin was one-sided and as charming as a troubadour's. It was echoed in his large, very blue eyes, and it quite entranced Meanne. He lowered his bundle from his shoulder.

"And did you know this hut was empty or did you come upon it by chance?"

"By chance," he said in an apologetic tone. "And you?"

"Know it was empty? I'd hoped it was," she said, looking about her at the mess. "But it isn't quite as I remembered it. Nor do I seem able to do anything about the state it's in." She allowed herself a deep, frustrated sigh.

"Being a lady, how would you know what it takes to set a hut to rights," he said, kindly but somewhat contemptuously. He went right to the fireplace and peered up the chimney. "It's blocked."

"That much I figured out for myself," she

16

said tartly.

"That's easy fixed."

"How?" She knew she sounded derisive.

"Leave it to Wisp, lady," he said as he darted out the door.

Almost the next instant she heard footsteps overhead, rather alarmingly heavy steps for so frail a boy: but then maybe the roof was not all that sturdy. Then there was a scraping noise echoing down the chimney. Curious, she peered up the flue and naturally got a face full of soot and the nests of the birds which had found the unused chimney an excellent place to build.

Coughing again, Meanne sternly kept her hands at her sides, not wanting to rub soot into her skin or her clothes—which would have to last her quite a while. She daren't open her eyes. She stood there, listening to Wisp's heavy footsteps on the roof, the remarkably loud thud he made, dropping to the ground outside the door before he reentered.

"Oh!"

The little word not only was apology but

17

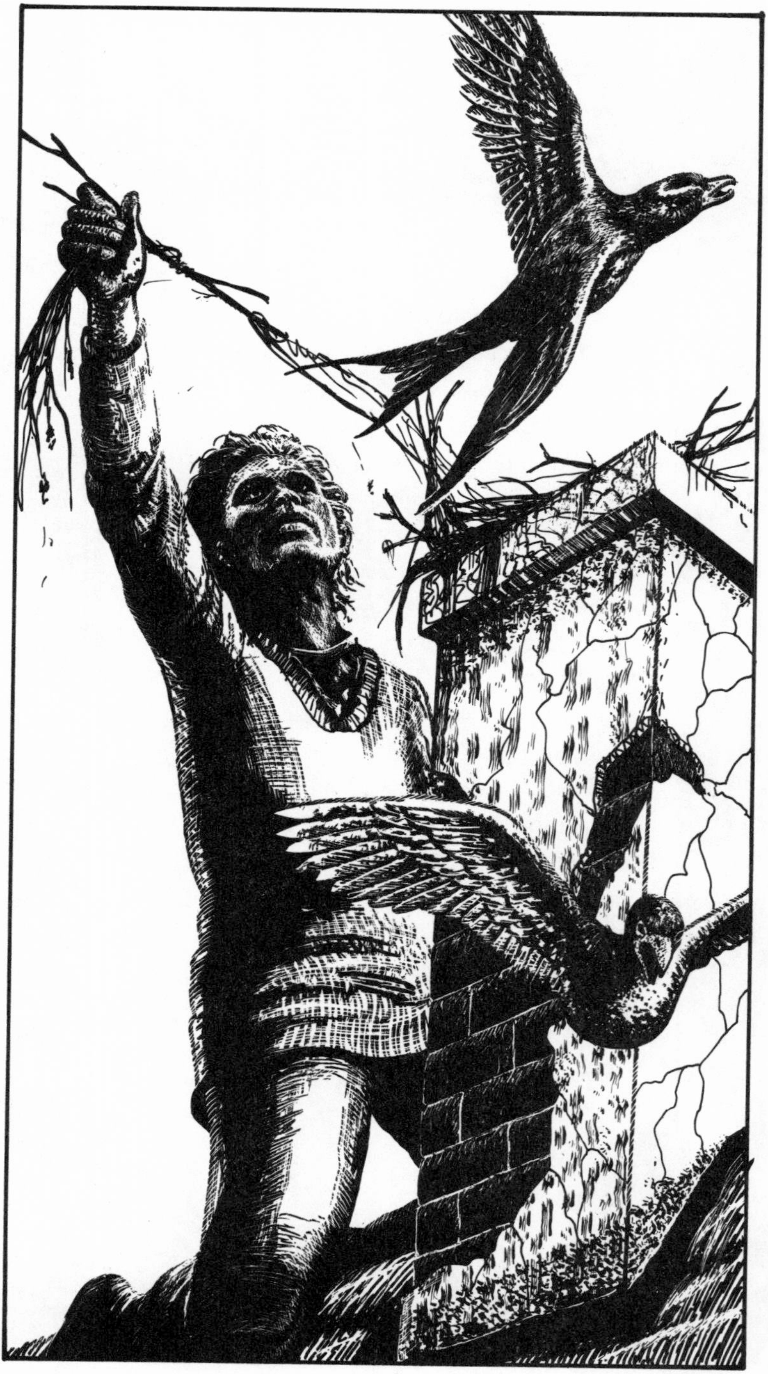

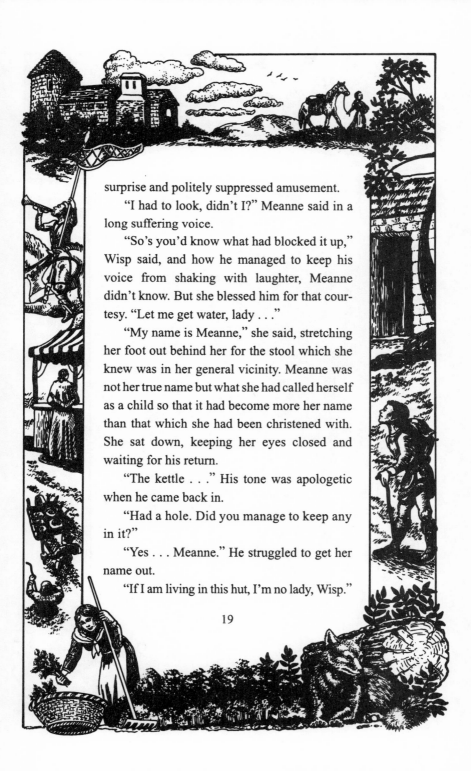

surprise and politely suppressed amusement.

"I had to look, didn't I?" Meanne said in a long suffering voice.

"So's you'd know what had blocked it up," Wisp said, and how he managed to keep his voice from shaking with laughter, Meanne didn't know. But she blessed him for that courtesy. "Let me get water, lady . . ."

"My name is Meanne," she said, stretching her foot out behind her for the stool which she knew was in her general vicinity. Meanne was not her true name but what she had called herself as a child so that it had become more her name than that which she had been christened with. She sat down, keeping her eyes closed and waiting for his return.

"The kettle . . ." His tone was apologetic when he came back in.

"Had a hole. Did you manage to keep any in it?"

"Yes . . . Meanne." He struggled to get her name out.

"If I am living in this hut, I'm no lady, Wisp."

19

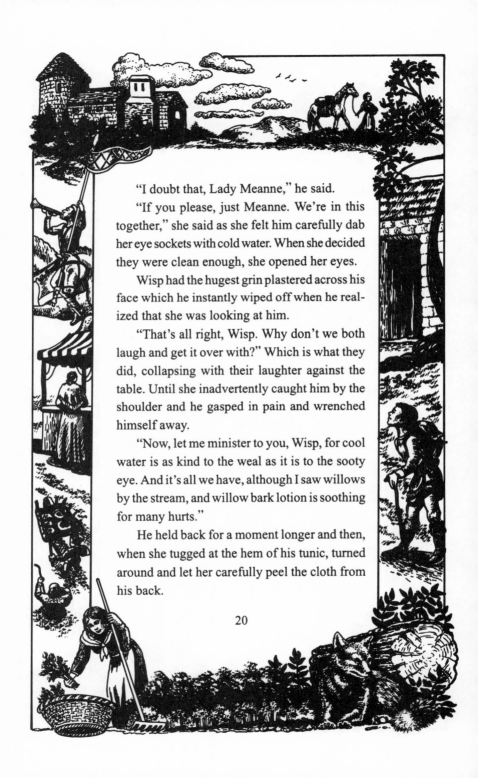

"I doubt that, Lady Meanne," he said.

"If you please, just Meanne. We're in this together," she said as she felt him carefully dab her eye sockets with cold water. When she decided they were clean enough, she opened her eyes.

Wisp had the hugest grin plastered across his face which he instantly wiped off when he realized that she was looking at him.

"That's all right, Wisp. Why don't we both laugh and get it over with?" Which is what they did, collapsing with their laughter against the table. Until she inadvertently caught him by the shoulder and he gasped in pain and wrenched himself away.

"Now, let me minister to you, Wisp, for cool water is as kind to the weal as it is to the sooty eye. And it's all we have, although I saw willows by the stream, and willow bark lotion is soothing for many hurts."

He held back for a moment longer and then, when she tugged at the hem of his tunic, turned around and let her carefully peel the cloth from his back.

20

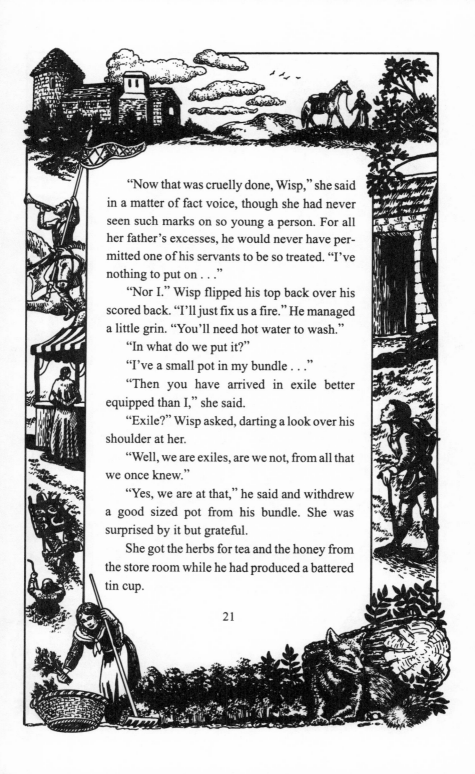

"Now that was cruelly done, Wisp," she said in a matter of fact voice, though she had never seen such marks on so young a person. For all her father's excesses, he would never have permitted one of his servants to be so treated. "I've nothing to put on . . ."

"Nor I." Wisp flipped his top back over his scored back. "I'll just fix us a fire." He managed a little grin. "You'll need hot water to wash."

"In what do we put it?"

"I've a small pot in my bundle . . ."

"Then you have arrived in exile better equipped than I," she said.

"Exile?" Wisp asked, darting a look over his shoulder at her.

"Well, we are exiles, are we not, from all that we once knew."

"Yes, we are at that," he said and withdrew a good sized pot from his bundle. She was surprised by it but grateful.

She got the herbs for tea and the honey from the store room while he had produced a battered tin cup.

21

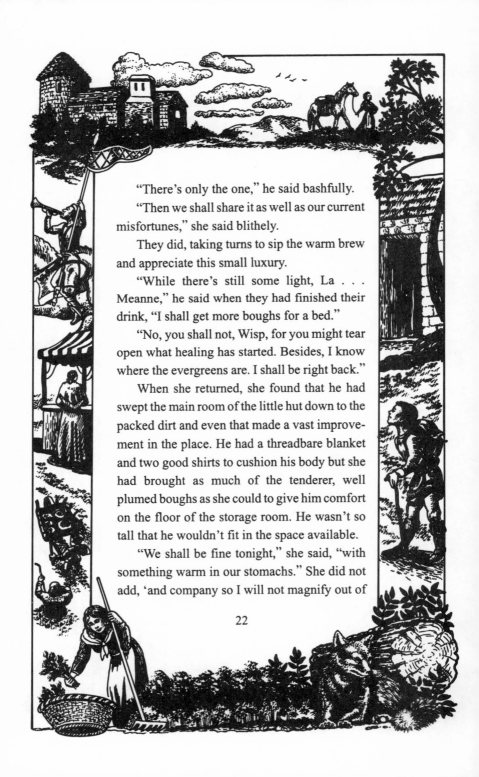

"There's only the one," he said bashfully.

"Then we shall share it as well as our current misfortunes," she said blithely.

They did, taking turns to sip the warm brew and appreciate this small luxury.

"While there's still some light, La . . . Meanne," he said when they had finished their drink, "I shall get more boughs for a bed."

"No, you shall not, Wisp, for you might tear open what healing has started. Besides, I know where the evergreens are. I shall be right back."

When she returned, she found that he had swept the main room of the little hut down to the packed dirt and even that made a vast improvement in the place. He had a threadbare blanket and two good shirts to cushion his body but she had brought as much of the tenderer, well plumed boughs as she could to give him comfort on the floor of the storage room. He wasn't so tall that he wouldn't fit in the space available.

"We shall be fine tonight," she said, "with something warm in our stomachs." She did not add, 'and company so I will not magnify out of

22

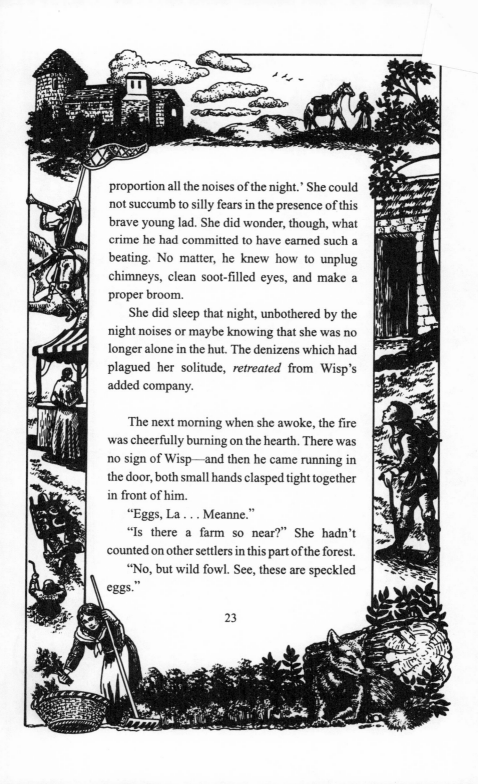

proportion all the noises of the night.' She could not succumb to silly fears in the presence of this brave young lad. She did wonder, though, what crime he had committed to have earned such a beating. No matter, he knew how to unplug chimneys, clean soot-filled eyes, and make a proper broom.

She did sleep that night, unbothered by the night noises or maybe knowing that she was no longer alone in the hut. The denizens which had plagued her solitude, *retreated* from Wisp's added company.

The next morning when she awoke, the fire was cheerfully burning on the hearth. There was no sign of Wisp—and then he came running in the door, both small hands clasped tight together in front of him.

"Eggs, La . . . Meanne."

"Is there a farm so near?" She hadn't counted on other settlers in this part of the forest.

"No, but wild fowl. See, these are speckled eggs."

23

"They'll taste as well speckles or not," she said, her mouth salivating for the treat. "Only," and now she groaned, "however will we cook them?"

He pointed to the flat rock balanced on the trivet just above the spritely fire. He must have done it before she got up. "It's hot enough to fry 'em now."

He knelt by the hearth and cracked the first one, which sizzled when it hit the stone. It was hot enough to keep the white from spreading far. When it was cooked, he carefully slid his knife blade beneath it, and then flipped it onto a piece of slate, which he handed to her.

"I scrubbed all the stones with sand from the stream, Meanne," he said. Then he turned back to cook his own egg.

"Never has hen fruit tasted so good," Meanne said, savoring her first forkful. "I think this will come in handy for you," she added, handing him the spoon she had filched.

"Food of the gods," he said with an unexpected display of panache and grinned so cockily at her that she could only laugh.

24

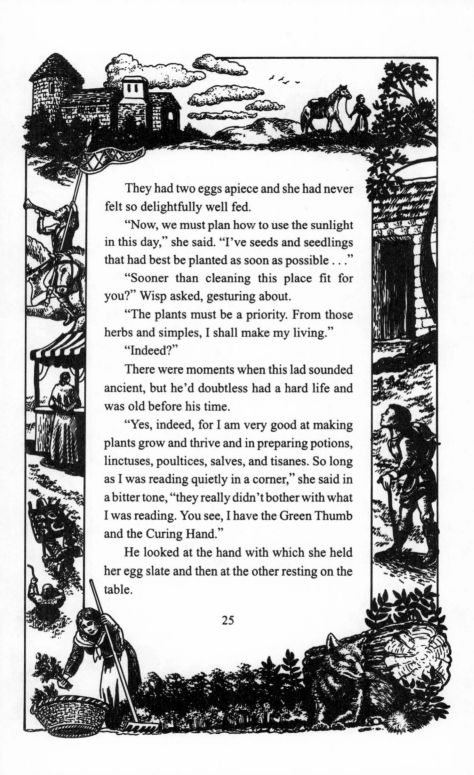

They had two eggs apiece and she had never felt so delightfully well fed.

"Now, we must plan how to use the sunlight in this day," she said. "I've seeds and seedlings that had best be planted as soon as possible . . ."

"Sooner than cleaning this place fit for you?" Wisp asked, gesturing about.

"The plants must be a priority. From those herbs and simples, I shall make my living."

"Indeed?"

There were moments when this lad sounded ancient, but he'd doubtless had a hard life and was old before his time.

"Yes, indeed, for I am very good at making plants grow and thrive and in preparing potions, linctuses, poultices, salves, and tisanes. So long as I was reading quietly in a corner," she said in a bitter tone, "they really didn't bother with what I was reading. You see, I have the Green Thumb and the Curing Hand."

He looked at the hand with which she held her egg slate and then at the other resting on the table.

25

"They don't look any different to mine."

"Ah, they don't have to look green," she said regarding both hands critically, "but in them lies my Gift, and they make green and abundant anything I choose to grow and potent anything I choose to prepare. So, I'll make ready the garden . . ."

"D'you know how, La . . . Meanne?" Wisp plainly had doubts on that score.

"Chimneys may defeat me, but gardens do not," she said firmly and got to her feet. "I have theory as well as practice." She didn't say that three window boxes in her own solar was the extent of her practice, but she knew her Gift would suffice.

"Then I shall assist . . ."

"Not with that sore back you don't . . ."

Wisp shrugged. "I'm not so poor I cannot help a lady."

"How often must I tell you that I'm not a lady here?"

"As you wish. I grant you it's not much of a place but, while you start your garden, I shall do

26

what I can to clean and set snares for woodcocks and rabbits. I saw their tracks."

"Is that your Gift?"

"My Gift?" and Wisp looked startled and then gave a little laugh. "No, that is not my Gift, though a useful one it would be. Not everyone has a Gift, you know," he added in a melancholy tone.

"Sadly that is true," she said, "but you have a sweet smile and a helpful disposition and those are sometimes more than many Gifted people have."

He swept her a passable and charming bow. He must have lived in a courtly house to have learned such a gesture, Meanne thought as she went to the window ledge to collect the seedlings.

Despite the tangles of weeds in the old garden, recent rains made the earth loose enough to pull them out easily. On her hands and knees, she prepared the ground, sifting through the moist dirt with her fingers to remove any stones that might have grown up in the patch since it

27

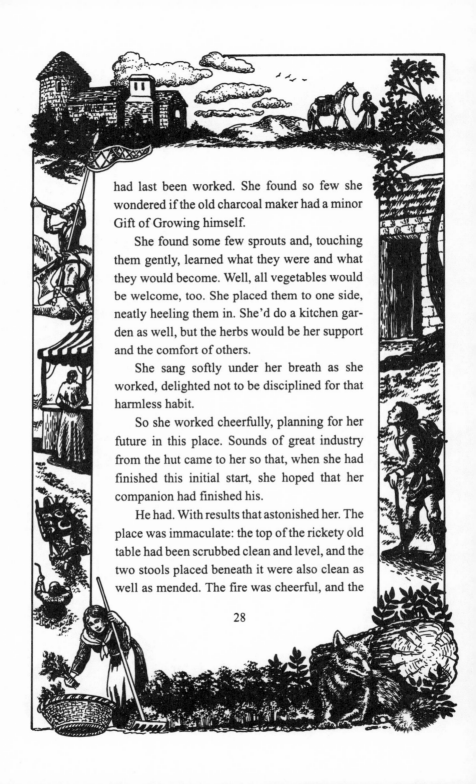

had last been worked. She found so few she wondered if the old charcoal maker had a minor Gift of Growing himself.

She found some few sprouts and, touching them gently, learned what they were and what they would become. Well, all vegetables would be welcome, too. She placed them to one side, neatly heeling them in. She'd do a kitchen garden as well, but the herbs would be her support and the comfort of others.

She sang softly under her breath as she worked, delighted not to be disciplined for that harmless habit.

So she worked cheerfully, planning for her future in this place. Sounds of great industry from the hut came to her so that, when she had finished this initial start, she hoped that her companion had finished his.

He had. With results that astonished her. The place was immaculate: the top of the rickety old table had been scrubbed clean and level, and the two stools placed beneath it were also clean as well as mended. The fire was cheerful, and the

28

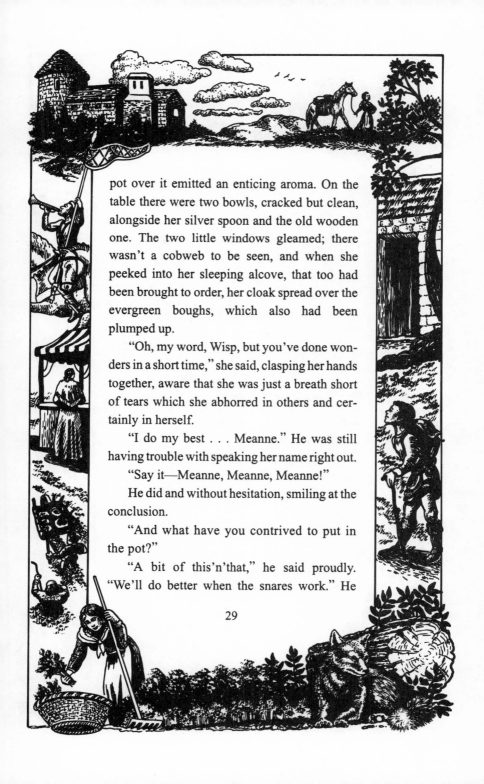

pot over it emitted an enticing aroma. On the table there were two bowls, cracked but clean, alongside her silver spoon and the old wooden one. The two little windows gleamed; there wasn't a cobweb to be seen, and when she peeked into her sleeping alcove, that too had been brought to order, her cloak spread over the evergreen boughs, which also had been plumped up.

"Oh, my word, Wisp, but you've done wonders in a short time," she said, clasping her hands together, aware that she was just a breath short of tears which she abhorred in others and certainly in herself.

"I do my best . . . Meanne." He was still having trouble with speaking her name right out.

"Say it—Meanne, Meanne, Meanne!"

He did and without hesitation, smiling at the conclusion.

"And what have you contrived to put in the pot?"

"A bit of this'n'that," he said proudly. "We'll do better when the snares work." He

29

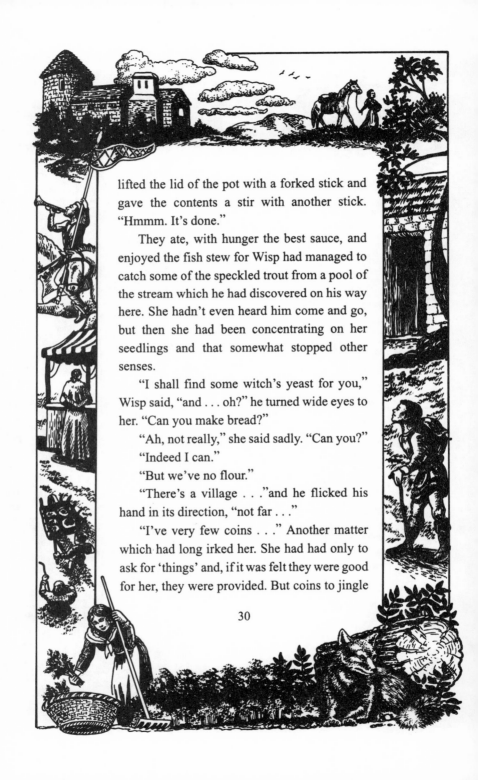

lifted the lid of the pot with a forked stick and gave the contents a stir with another stick. "Hmmm. It's done."

They ate, with hunger the best sauce, and enjoyed the fish stew for Wisp had managed to catch some of the speckled trout from a pool of the stream which he had discovered on his way here. She hadn't even heard him come and go, but then she had been concentrating on her seedlings and that somewhat stopped other senses.

"I shall find some witch's yeast for you," Wisp said, "and . . . oh?" he turned wide eyes to her. "Can you make bread?"

"Ah, not really," she said sadly. "Can you?"

"Indeed I can."

"But we've no flour."

"There's a village . . ."and he flicked his hand in its direction, "not far . . ."

"I've very few coins . . ." Another matter which had long irked her. She had had only to ask for 'things' and, if it was felt they were good for her, they were provided. But coins to jingle

30

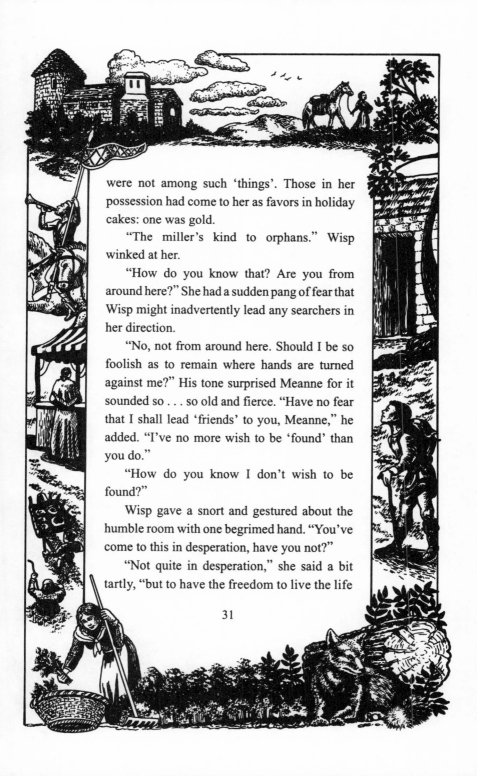

were not among such 'things'. Those in her possession had come to her as favors in holiday cakes: one was gold.

"The miller's kind to orphans." Wisp winked at her.

"How do you know that? Are you from around here?" She had a sudden pang of fear that Wisp might inadvertently lead any searchers in her direction.

"No, not from around here. Should I be so foolish as to remain where hands are turned against me?" His tone surprised Meanne for it sounded so . . . so old and fierce. "Have no fear that I shall lead 'friends' to you, Meanne," he added. "I've no more wish to be 'found' than you do."

"How do you know I don't wish to be found?"

Wisp gave a snort and gestured about the humble room with one begrimed hand. "You've come to this in desperation, have you not?"

"Not quite in desperation," she said a bit tartly, "but to have the freedom to live the life

31

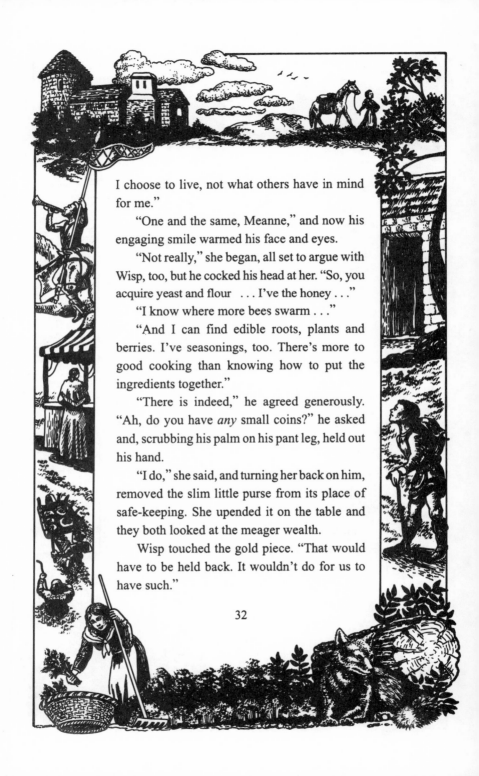

I choose to live, not what others have in mind for me."

"One and the same, Meanne," and now his engaging smile warmed his face and eyes.

"Not really," she began, all set to argue with Wisp, too, but he cocked his head at her. "So, you acquire yeast and flour . . . I've the honey . . ."

"I know where more bees swarm . . ."

"And I can find edible roots, plants and berries. I've seasonings, too. There's more to good cooking than knowing how to put the ingredients together."

"There is indeed," he agreed generously. "Ah, do you have *any* small coins?" he asked and, scrubbing his palm on his pant leg, held out his hand.

"I do," she said, and turning her back on him, removed the slim little purse from its place of safe-keeping. She upended it on the table and they both looked at the meager wealth.

Wisp touched the gold piece. "That would have to be held back. It wouldn't do for us to have such."

32

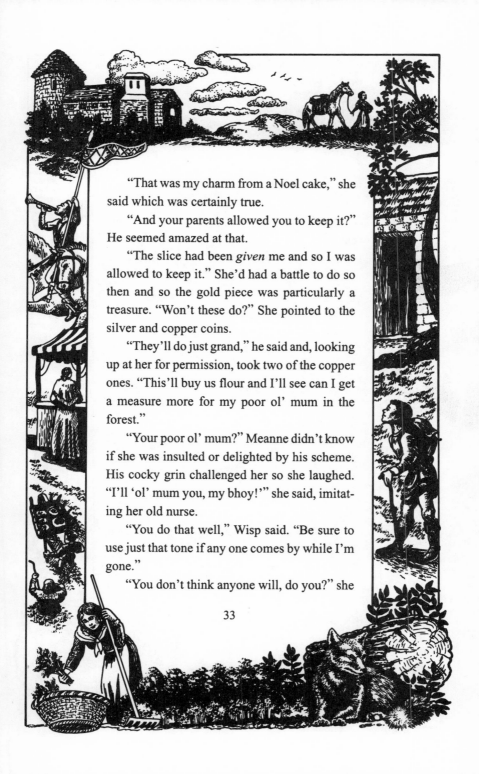

"That was my charm from a Noel cake," she said which was certainly true.

"And your parents allowed you to keep it?" He seemed amazed at that.

"The slice had been *given* me and so I was allowed to keep it." She'd had a battle to do so then and so the gold piece was particularly a treasure. "Won't these do?" She pointed to the silver and copper coins.

"They'll do just grand," he said and, looking up at her for permission, took two of the copper ones. "This'll buy us flour and I'll see can I get a measure more for my poor ol' mum in the forest."

"Your poor ol' mum?" Meanne didn't know if she was insulted or delighted by his scheme. His cocky grin challenged her so she laughed. "I'll 'ol' mum you, my bhoy!'" she said, imitating her old nurse.

"You do that well," Wisp said. "Be sure to use just that tone if any one comes by while I'm gone."

"You don't think anyone will, do you?" she

33

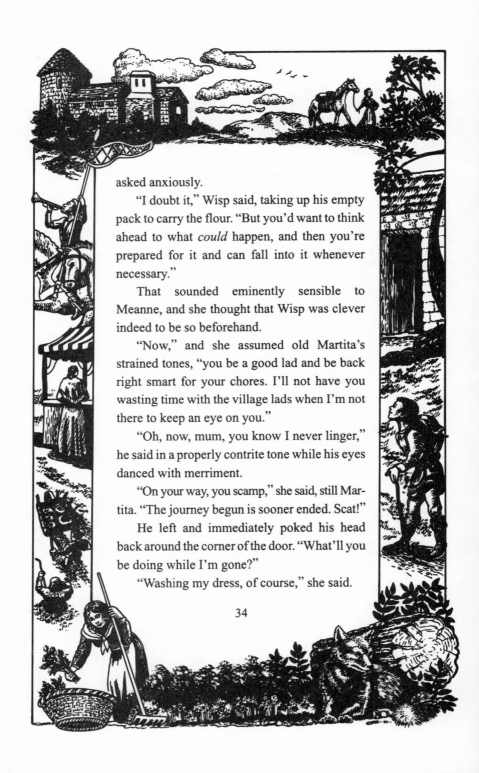

asked anxiously.

"I doubt it," Wisp said, taking up his empty pack to carry the flour. "But you'd want to think ahead to what *could* happen, and then you're prepared for it and can fall into it whenever necessary."

That sounded eminently sensible to Meanne, and she thought that Wisp was clever indeed to be so beforehand.

"Now," and she assumed old Martita's strained tones, "you be a good lad and be back right smart for your chores. I'll not have you wasting time with the village lads when I'm not there to keep an eye on you."

"Oh, now, mum, you know I never linger," he said in a properly contrite tone while his eyes danced with merriment.

"On your way, you scamp," she said, still Martita. "The journey begun is sooner ended. Scat!"

He left and immediately poked his head back around the corner of the door. "What'll you be doing while I'm gone?"

"Washing my dress, of course," she said.

34

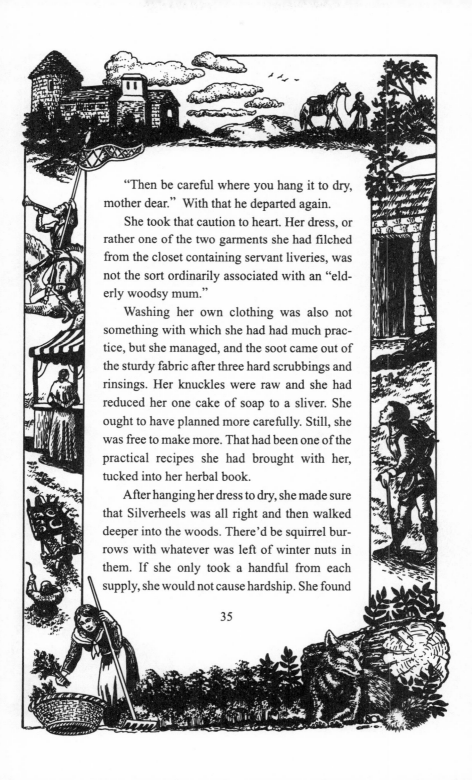

"Then be careful where you hang it to dry, mother dear." With that he departed again.

She took that caution to heart. Her dress, or rather one of the two garments she had filched from the closet containing servant liveries, was not the sort ordinarily associated with an "elderly woodsy mum."

Washing her own clothing was also not something with which she had had much practice, but she managed, and the soot came out of the sturdy fabric after three hard scrubbings and rinsings. Her knuckles were raw and she had reduced her one cake of soap to a sliver. She ought to have planned more carefully. Still, she was free to make more. That had been one of the practical recipes she had brought with her, tucked into her herbal book.

After hanging her dress to dry, she made sure that Silverheels was all right and then walked deeper into the woods. There'd be squirrel burrows with whatever was left of winter nuts in them. If she only took a handful from each supply, she would not cause hardship. She found

35

mushrooms as well, the big capped ones, and filled her skirt on her way back to the hut. And she plucked a handful of bluebells and cowslips. Flowers did so brighten a place.

That evening Wisp taught her how to make bread for he'd been given a start of yeast by the miller's wife. He'd found duck eggs on his way back and collected two woodcocks from his snares. So they feasted.

"They've a market fair every month, the first Saturday," Wisp told her as he picked clean the bones of his bird. "When you've herbs and all to be sold, that'd be a good place to go."

"I think not," Meanne said.

"Oh? Well, I can come and go. No one pays much attention to a scamp like me," Wisp said, his charming grin in place. "But you'll want to, sooner or later."

"No, I won't. I'm safe here."

"You'll be safe with me at the market, too."

"I may be able to sound like an old crone from the safety of this hut," she said spiritedly,

36

"but I *know* I don't look like one. Yet."

"That you do not, Lady Meanne, but with a little coaching from me," and his grin was malicious, "I can school you to assume the character that's needed. A little dirt on your face, some soot in your hair . . ." and he hastily added, "though it's a shame to do so . . . You'll be safe enough . . . me ol' mum!"

"I doubt I'll feel the need for company."

"Thank you, Meanne," he said.

"I didn't mean to compliment you, you young scamp."

"But you did!" He waggled a finger at her, very pleased with himself.

"And tomorrow we'll have no scivving off to the village to gossip and . . ."

"Gossip I didn't, Meanne, but I did get us a bit of butter for our bread."

"Oh, you didn't!" Meanne felt her mouth salivating for bread and butter even though her stomach was remarkably full. She'd forgot how she missed such commonplaces. "Now, about tomorrow," she said, bringing herself back to the

37

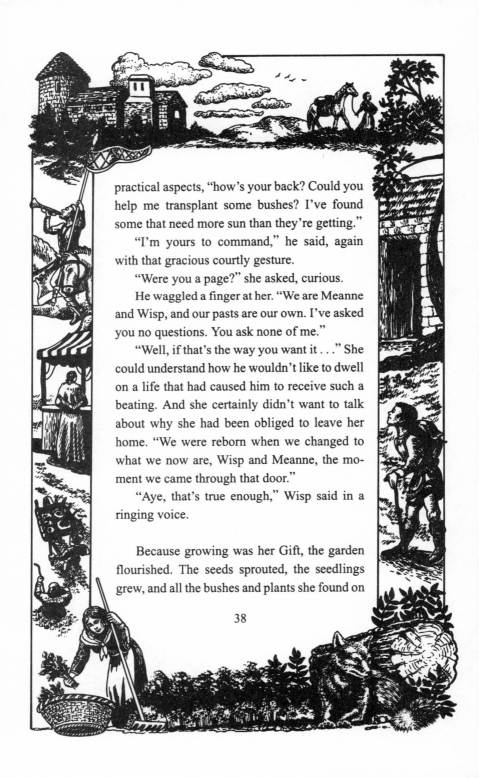

practical aspects, "how's your back? Could you help me transplant some bushes? I've found some that need more sun than they're getting."

"I'm yours to command," he said, again with that gracious courtly gesture.

"Were you a page?" she asked, curious.

He waggled a finger at her. "We are Meanne and Wisp, and our pasts are our own. I've asked you no questions. You ask none of me."

"Well, if that's the way you want it . . ." She could understand how he wouldn't like to dwell on a life that had caused him to receive such a beating. And she certainly didn't want to talk about why she had been obliged to leave her home. "We were reborn when we changed to what we now are, Wisp and Meanne, the moment we came through that door."

"Aye, that's true enough," Wisp said in a ringing voice.

Because growing was her Gift, the garden flourished. The seeds sprouted, the seedlings grew, and all the bushes and plants she found on

38

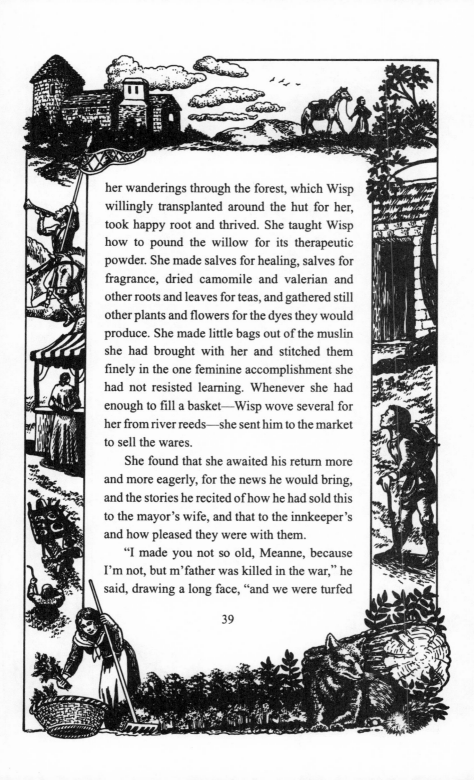

her wanderings through the forest, which Wisp
willingly transplanted around the hut for her,
took happy root and thrived. She taught Wisp
how to pound the willow for its therapeutic
powder. She made salves for healing, salves for
fragrance, dried camomile and valerian and
other roots and leaves for teas, and gathered still
other plants and flowers for the dyes they would
produce. She made little bags out of the muslin
she had brought with her and stitched them
finely in the one feminine accomplishment she
had not resisted learning. Whenever she had
enough to fill a basket—Wisp wove several for
her from river reeds—she sent him to the market
to sell the wares.

She found that she awaited his return more
and more eagerly, for the news he would bring,
and the stories he recited of how he had sold this
to the mayor's wife, and that to the innkeeper's
and how pleased they were with them.

"I made you not so old, Meanne, because
I'm not, but m'father was killed in the war," he
said, drawing a long face, "and we were turfed

39

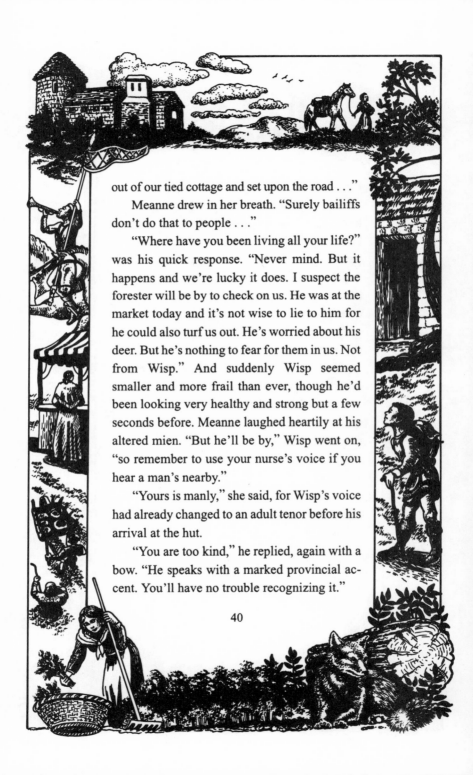

out of our tied cottage and set upon the road . . ."

Meanne drew in her breath. "Surely bailiffs don't do that to people . . ."

"Where have you been living all your life?" was his quick response. "Never mind. But it happens and we're lucky it does. I suspect the forester will be by to check on us. He was at the market today and it's not wise to lie to him for he could also turf us out. He's worried about his deer. But he's nothing to fear for them in us. Not from Wisp." And suddenly Wisp seemed smaller and more frail than ever, though he'd been looking very healthy and strong but a few seconds before. Meanne laughed heartily at his altered mien. "But he'll be by," Wisp went on, "so remember to use your nurse's voice if you hear a man's nearby."

"Yours is manly," she said, for Wisp's voice had already changed to an adult tenor before his arrival at the hut.

"You are too kind," he replied, again with a bow. "He speaks with a marked provincial accent. You'll have no trouble recognizing it."

40

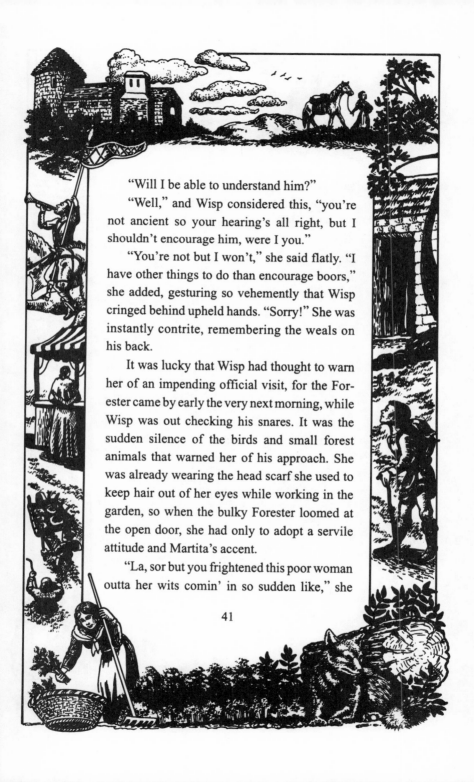

"Will I be able to understand him?"

"Well," and Wisp considered this, "you're not ancient so your hearing's all right, but I shouldn't encourage him, were I you."

"You're not but I won't," she said flatly. "I have other things to do than encourage boors," she added, gesturing so vehemently that Wisp cringed behind upheld hands. "Sorry!" She was instantly contrite, remembering the weals on his back.

It was lucky that Wisp had thought to warn her of an impending official visit, for the Forester came by early the very next morning, while Wisp was out checking his snares. It was the sudden silence of the birds and small forest animals that warned her of his approach. She was already wearing the head scarf she used to keep hair out of her eyes while working in the garden, so when the bulky Forester loomed at the open door, she had only to adopt a servile attitude and Martita's accent.

"La, sor but you frightened this poor woman outta her wits comin' in so sudden like," she

41

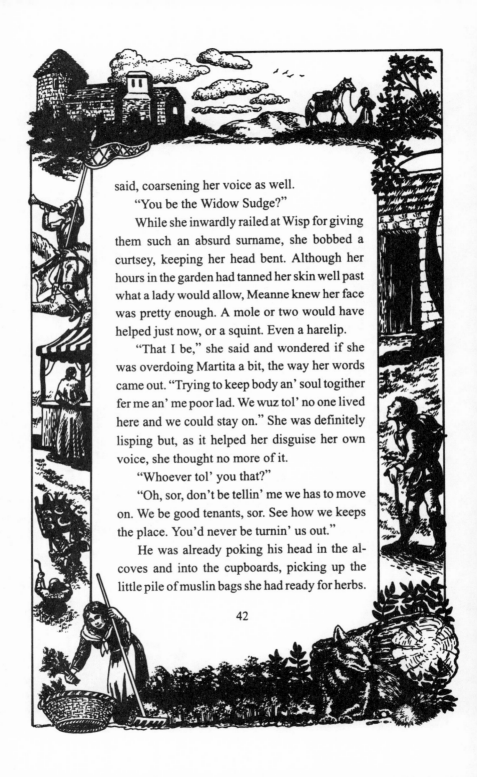

said, coarsening her voice as well.

"You be the Widow Sudge?"

While she inwardly railed at Wisp for giving them such an absurd surname, she bobbed a curtsey, keeping her head bent. Although her hours in the garden had tanned her skin well past what a lady would allow, Meanne knew her face was pretty enough. A mole or two would have helped just now, or a squint. Even a harelip.

"That I be," she said and wondered if she was overdoing Martita a bit, the way her words came out. "Trying to keep body an' soul togither fer me an' me poor lad. We wuz tol' no one lived here and we could stay on." She was definitely lisping but, as it helped her disguise her own voice, she thought no more of it.

"Whoever tol' you that?"

"Oh, sor, don't be tellin' me we has to move on. We be good tenants, sor. See how we keeps the place. You'd never be turnin' us out."

He was already poking his head in the alcoves and into the cupboards, picking up the little pile of muslin bags she had ready for herbs.

She and Wisp had hidden their small store of coins under a loose brick in the wall of her sleeping place, though the gold one remained in her bodice.

"Neat it is, I see, Widow, an' if you'd a coin or two for rent, why I could see my way clear to turn my head from your ock-cue-pay-shun. That is," and he held up a hand, "'til I can find someone else to make charcoal. You being the widow of a war hero who'd won three medals for valor . . ." And he gave her a quick look, and as quickly away as if he couldn't bear looking at her.

"Oh, sor, we've so little . . ."

"That son of yours did a brisk trade at the market yesterday, Widow Sudge." He cocked his head at her, his eye knowing.

"Oh, we've little enough for all of that," she began, moaning, and not knowing how to forestall him, "and my son keeps it by him . . ."

"Then we'll wait for his return," the Forester said, pulling one of the stools out from under the table with a deft hook of his foot. And

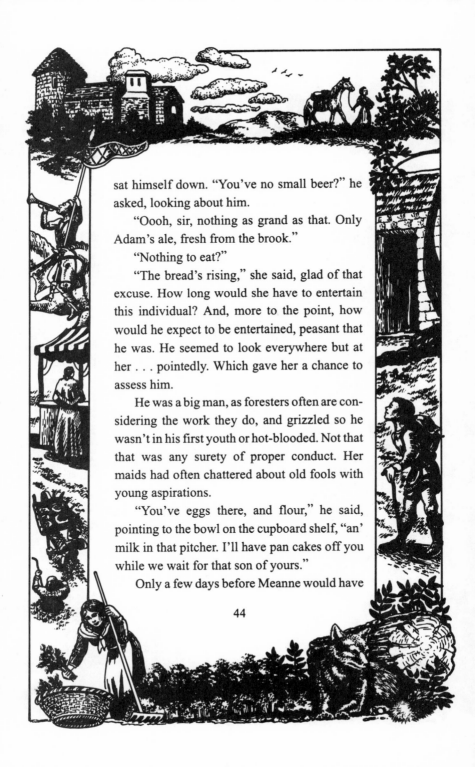

sat himself down. "You've no small beer?" he asked, looking about him.

"Oooh, sir, nothing as grand as that. Only Adam's ale, fresh from the brook."

"Nothing to eat?"

"The bread's rising," she said, glad of that excuse. How long would she have to entertain this individual? And, more to the point, how would he expect to be entertained, peasant that he was. He seemed to look everywhere but at her . . . pointedly. Which gave her a chance to assess him.

He was a big man, as foresters often are considering the work they do, and grizzled so he wasn't in his first youth or hot-blooded. Not that that was any surety of proper conduct. Her maids had often chattered about old fools with young aspirations.

"You've eggs there, and flour," he said, pointing to the bowl on the cupboard shelf, "an' milk in that pitcher. I'll have pan cakes off you while we wait for that son of yours."

Only a few days before Meanne would have

44

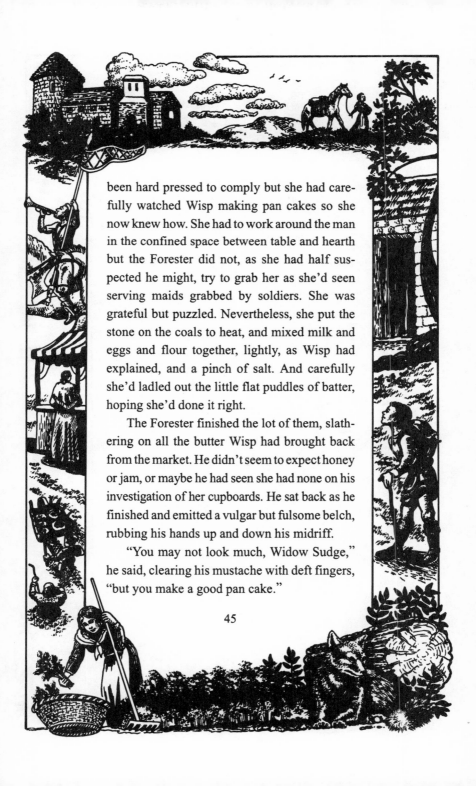

been hard pressed to comply but she had carefully watched Wisp making pan cakes so she now knew how. She had to work around the man in the confined space between table and hearth but the Forester did not, as she had half suspected he might, try to grab her as she'd seen serving maids grabbed by soldiers. She was grateful but puzzled. Nevertheless, she put the stone on the coals to heat, and mixed milk and eggs and flour together, lightly, as Wisp had explained, and a pinch of salt. And carefully she'd ladled out the little flat puddles of batter, hoping she'd done it right.

The Forester finished the lot of them, slathering on all the butter Wisp had brought back from the market. He didn't seem to expect honey or jam, or maybe he had seen she had none on his investigation of her cupboards. He sat back as he finished and emitted a vulgar but fulsome belch, rubbing his hands up and down his midriff.

"You may not look much, Widow Sudge," he said, clearing his mustache with deft fingers, "but you make a good pan cake."

45

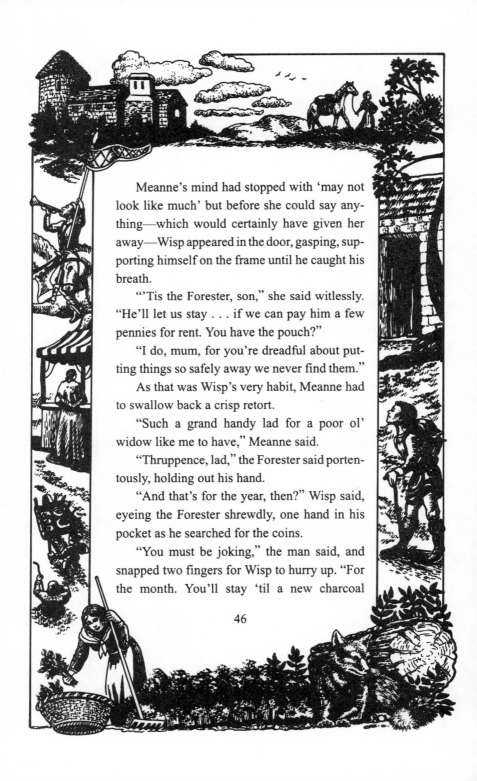

Meanne's mind had stopped with 'may not look like much' but before she could say anything—which would certainly have given her away—Wisp appeared in the door, gasping, supporting himself on the frame until he caught his breath.

"'Tis the Forester, son," she said witlessly. "He'll let us stay . . . if we can pay him a few pennies for rent. You have the pouch?"

"I do, mum, for you're dreadful about putting things so safely away we never find them."

As that was Wisp's very habit, Meanne had to swallow back a crisp retort.

"Such a grand handy lad for a poor ol' widow like me to have," Meanne said.

"Thruppence, lad," the Forester said portentously, holding out his hand.

"And that's for the year, then?" Wisp said, eyeing the Forester shrewdly, one hand in his pocket as he searched for the coins.

"You must be joking," the man said, and snapped two fingers for Wisp to hurry up. "For the month. You'll stay 'til a new charcoal

46

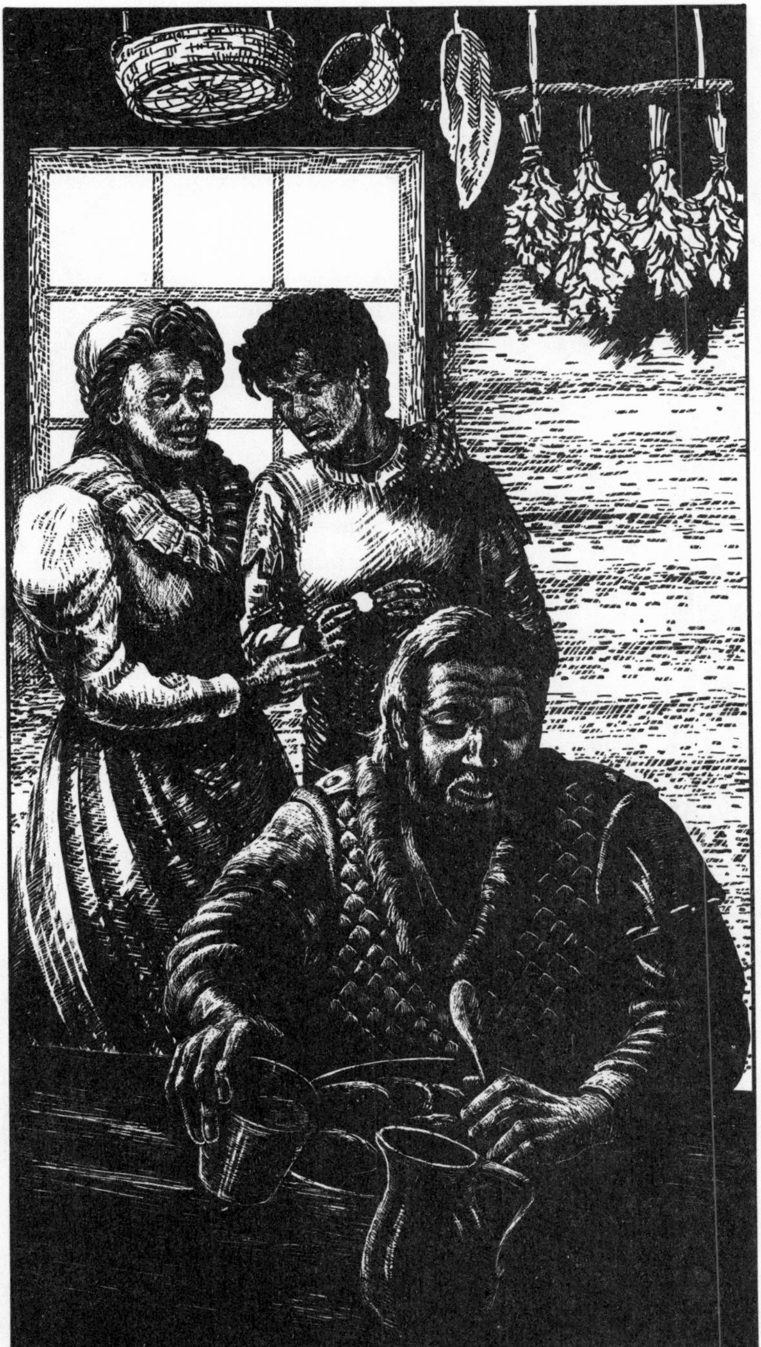

maker's found and lucky at that."

"Oh, we are, your honor," Meanne said though she longed to prick his consequence somehow or other. "Lucky indeed to have a roof over our heads an' all."

Wisp finally located the coins and, as he drew them out of his pocket, Meanne gasped for they looked more like the flat pebbles a boy would skip over the water than pennies. She had been mistaken for they clinked into the Forester's hand.

He rose then and, without a backward glance, retrieved the big axe he had left at the door, striding away into the woods as if he, not the Lord, owned them.

When Meanne looked back at Wisp, he had both hands over his mouth, choking back his laughter.

"It's no laughing matter, Wisp," she said, hands on her hips, incensed that the Forester had had not only a good meal but three pennies from them in the same day. "He ate half the flour you brought back."

48

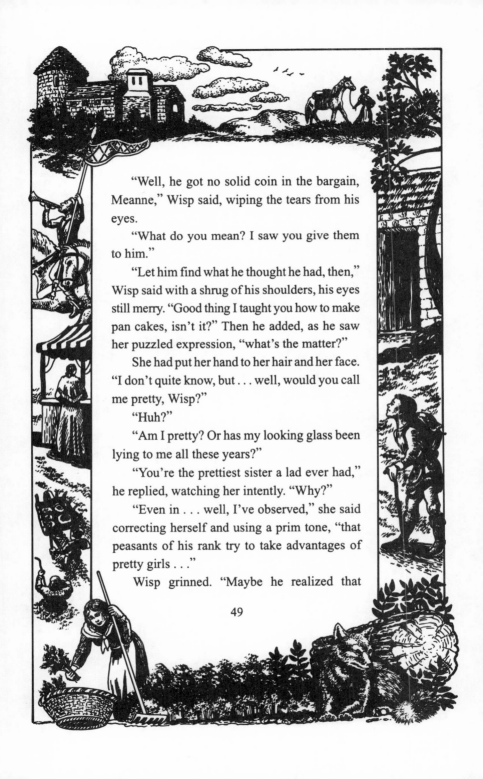

"Well, he got no solid coin in the bargain, Meanne," Wisp said, wiping the tears from his eyes.

"What do you mean? I saw you give them to him."

"Let him find what he thought he had, then," Wisp said with a shrug of his shoulders, his eyes still merry. "Good thing I taught you how to make pan cakes, isn't it?" Then he added, as he saw her puzzled expression, "what's the matter?"

She had put her hand to her hair and her face. "I don't quite know, but . . . well, would you call me pretty, Wisp?"

"Huh?"

"Am I pretty? Or has my looking glass been lying to me all these years?"

"You're the prettiest sister a lad ever had," he replied, watching her intently. "Why?"

"Even in . . . well, I've observed," she said correcting herself and using a prim tone, "that peasants of his rank try to take advantages of pretty girls . . ."

Wisp grinned. "Maybe he realized that

49

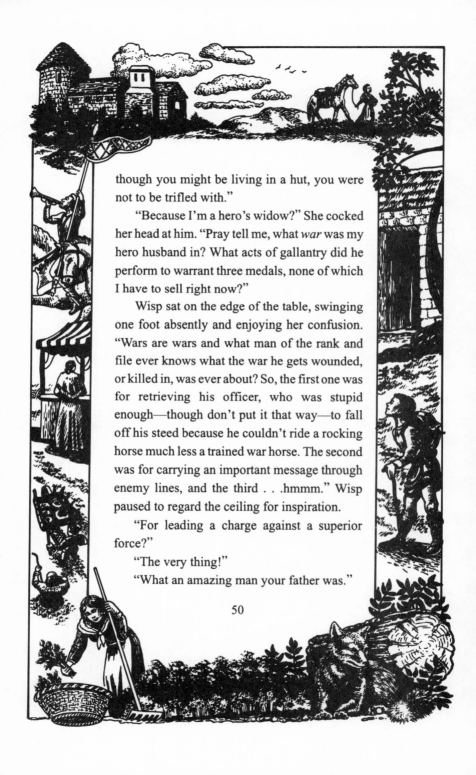

though you might be living in a hut, you were not to be trifled with."

"Because I'm a hero's widow?" She cocked her head at him. "Pray tell me, what *war* was my hero husband in? What acts of gallantry did he perform to warrant three medals, none of which I have to sell right now?"

Wisp sat on the edge of the table, swinging one foot absently and enjoying her confusion. "Wars are wars and what man of the rank and file ever knows what the war he gets wounded, or killed in, was ever about? So, the first one was for retrieving his officer, who was stupid enough—though don't put it that way—to fall off his steed because he couldn't ride a rocking horse much less a trained war horse. The second was for carrying an important message through enemy lines, and the third . . .hmmm." Wisp paused to regard the ceiling for inspiration.

"For leading a charge against a superior force?"

"The very thing!"

"What an amazing man your father was."

50

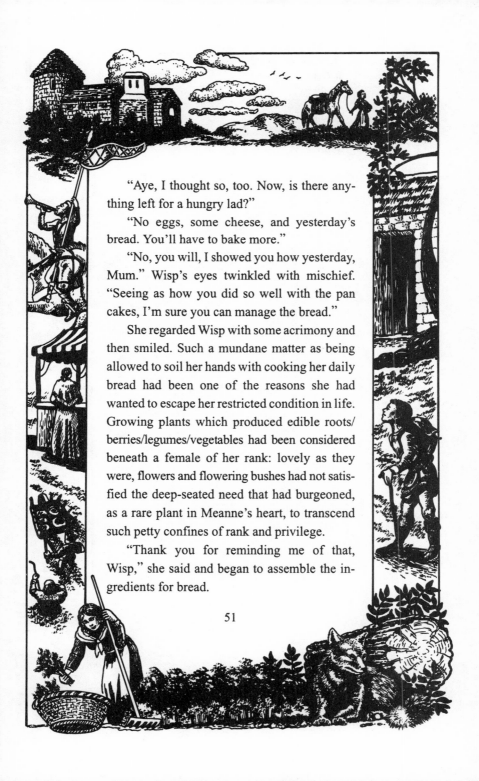

"Aye, I thought so, too. Now, is there anything left for a hungry lad?"

"No eggs, some cheese, and yesterday's bread. You'll have to bake more."

"No, you will, I showed you how yesterday, Mum." Wisp's eyes twinkled with mischief. "Seeing as how you did so well with the pan cakes, I'm sure you can manage the bread."

She regarded Wisp with some acrimony and then smiled. Such a mundane matter as being allowed to soil her hands with cooking her daily bread had been one of the reasons she had wanted to escape her restricted condition in life. Growing plants which produced edible roots/berries/legumes/vegetables had been considered beneath a female of her rank: lovely as they were, flowers and flowering bushes had not satisfied the deep-seated need that had burgeoned, as a rare plant in Meanne's heart, to transcend such petty confines of rank and privilege.

"Thank you for reminding me of that, Wisp," she said and began to assemble the ingredients for bread.

51

By evening she had four fine loaves, though a tad scorched because she was still refining her skill in using the wall oven. But she was improving.

"What will happen," she asked Wisp as they ate their simple meal, "when the Forester discovers he has lost the 'pennies'?"

"I suspect he might come back," Wisp said casually, "but I don't think he'll find the place right off."

"He found it easily enough this morning," Meanne said. "Can you not stay close in case I need you?"

"I could," Wisp said, "but I won't need to."

And he smiled that knowing smile that often made him appear much more adult than his years.

Meanne was not totally reassured and found herself very wakeful that night, fretting over how to cope with the hungers of the Forester as well as his anger at being duped. Finally, she got up to infuse a cup of camomile for herself. There

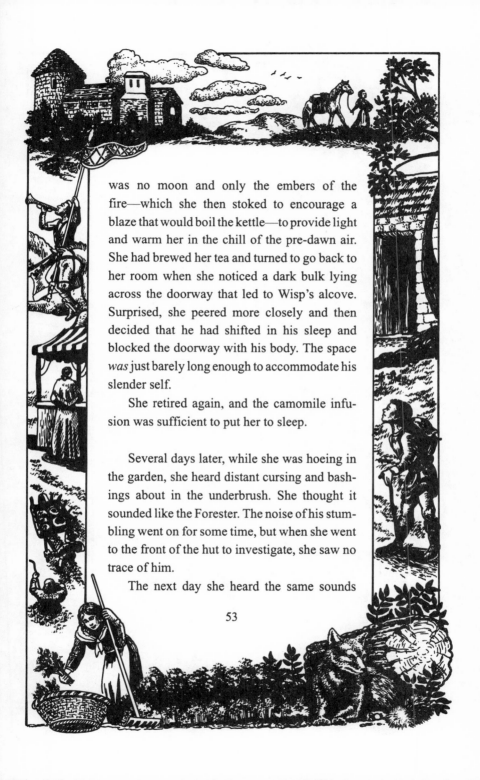

was no moon and only the embers of the fire—which she then stoked to encourage a blaze that would boil the kettle—to provide light and warm her in the chill of the pre-dawn air. She had brewed her tea and turned to go back to her room when she noticed a dark bulk lying across the doorway that led to Wisp's alcove. Surprised, she peered more closely and then decided that he had shifted in his sleep and blocked the doorway with his body. The space *was* just barely long enough to accommodate his slender self.

She retired again, and the camomile infusion was sufficient to put her to sleep.

Several days later, while she was hoeing in the garden, she heard distant cursing and bashings about in the underbrush. She thought it sounded like the Forester. The noise of his stumbling went on for some time, but when she went to the front of the hut to investigate, she saw no trace of him.

The next day she heard the same sounds

53

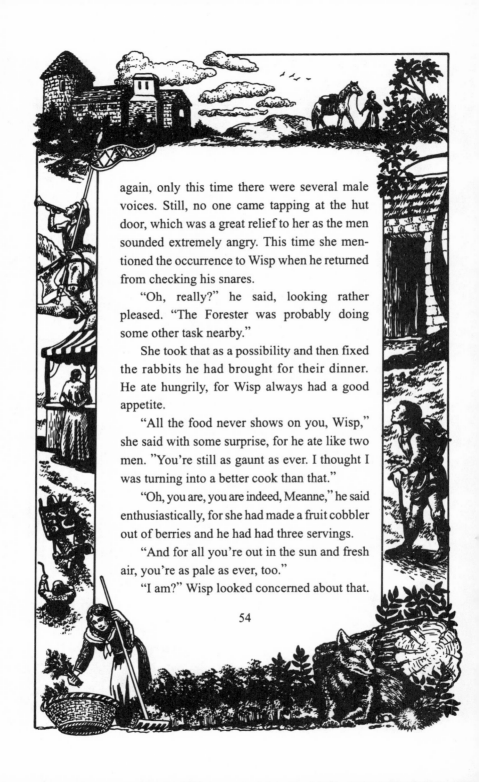

again, only this time there were several male voices. Still, no one came tapping at the hut door, which was a great relief to her as the men sounded extremely angry. This time she mentioned the occurrence to Wisp when he returned from checking his snares.

"Oh, really?" he said, looking rather pleased. "The Forester was probably doing some other task nearby."

She took that as a possibility and then fixed the rabbits he had brought for their dinner. He ate hungrily, for Wisp always had a good appetite.

"All the food never shows on you, Wisp," she said with some surprise, for he ate like two men. "You're still as gaunt as ever. I thought I was turning into a better cook than that."

"Oh, you are, you are indeed, Meanne," he said enthusiastically, for she had made a fruit cobbler out of berries and he had had three servings.

"And for all you're out in the sun and fresh air, you're as pale as ever, too."

"I am?" Wisp looked concerned about that.

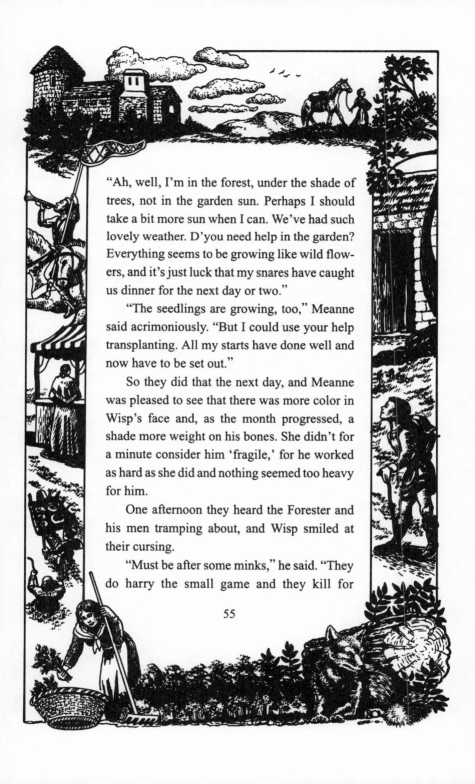

"Ah, well, I'm in the forest, under the shade of trees, not in the garden sun. Perhaps I should take a bit more sun when I can. We've had such lovely weather. D'you need help in the garden? Everything seems to be growing like wild flowers, and it's just luck that my snares have caught us dinner for the next day or two."

"The seedlings are growing, too," Meanne said acrimoniously. "But I could use your help transplanting. All my starts have done well and now have to be set out."

So they did that the next day, and Meanne was pleased to see that there was more color in Wisp's face and, as the month progressed, a shade more weight on his bones. She didn't for a minute consider him 'fragile,' for he worked as hard as she did and nothing seemed too heavy for him.

One afternoon they heard the Forester and his men tramping about, and Wisp smiled at their cursing.

"Must be after some minks," he said. "They do harry the small game and they kill for

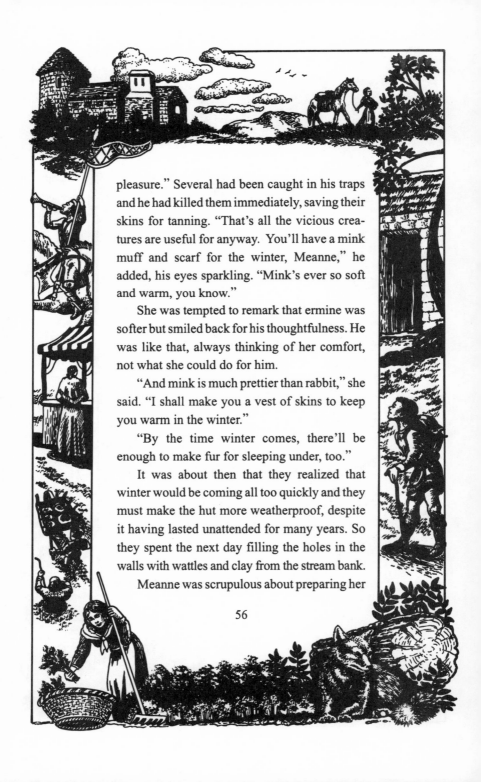

pleasure." Several had been caught in his traps and he had killed them immediately, saving their skins for tanning. "That's all the vicious creatures are useful for anyway. You'll have a mink muff and scarf for the winter, Meanne," he added, his eyes sparkling. "Mink's ever so soft and warm, you know."

She was tempted to remark that ermine was softer but smiled back for his thoughtfulness. He was like that, always thinking of her comfort, not what she could do for him.

"And mink is much prettier than rabbit," she said. "I shall make you a vest of skins to keep you warm in the winter."

"By the time winter comes, there'll be enough to make fur for sleeping under, too."

It was about then that they realized that winter would be coming all too quickly and they must make the hut more weatherproof, despite it having lasted unattended for many years. So they spent the next day filling the holes in the walls with wattles and clay from the stream bank.

Meanne was scrupulous about preparing her

56

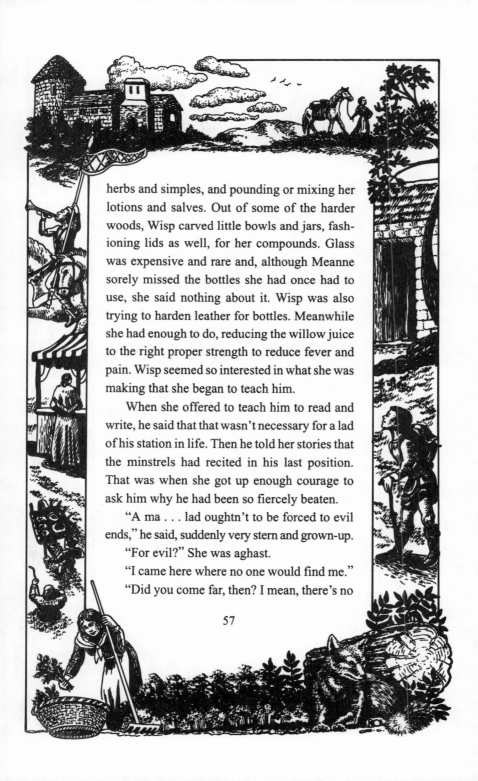

herbs and simples, and pounding or mixing her
lotions and salves. Out of some of the harder
woods, Wisp carved little bowls and jars, fash-
ioning lids as well, for her compounds. Glass
was expensive and rare and, although Meanne
sorely missed the bottles she had once had to
use, she said nothing about it. Wisp was also
trying to harden leather for bottles. Meanwhile
she had enough to do, reducing the willow juice
to the right proper strength to reduce fever and
pain. Wisp seemed so interested in what she was
making that she began to teach him.

When she offered to teach him to read and
write, he said that that wasn't necessary for a lad
of his station in life. Then he told her stories that
the minstrels had recited in his last position.
That was when she got up enough courage to
ask him why he had been so fiercely beaten.

"A ma . . . lad oughtn't to be forced to evil
ends," he said, suddenly very stern and grown-up.

"For evil?" She was aghast.

"I came here where no one would find me."

"Did you come far, then? I mean, there's no

57

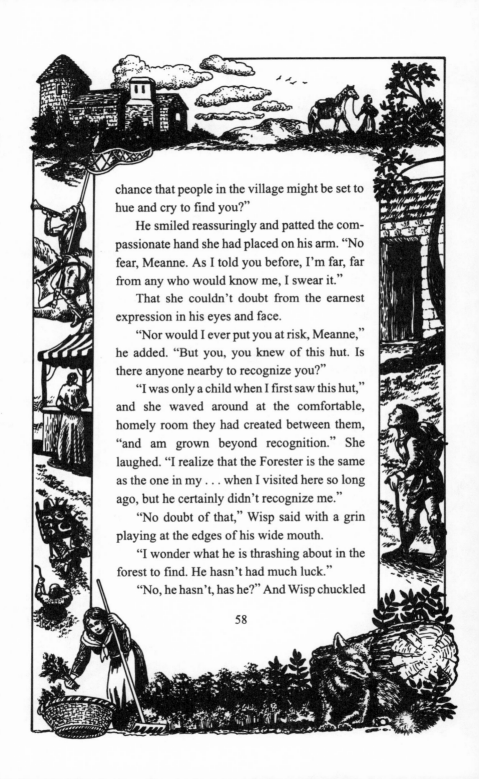

chance that people in the village might be set to hue and cry to find you?"

He smiled reassuringly and patted the compassionate hand she had placed on his arm. "No fear, Meanne. As I told you before, I'm far, far from any who would know me, I swear it."

That she couldn't doubt from the earnest expression in his eyes and face.

"Nor would I ever put you at risk, Meanne," he added. "But you, you knew of this hut. Is there anyone nearby to recognize you?"

"I was only a child when I first saw this hut," and she waved around at the comfortable, homely room they had created between them, "and am grown beyond recognition." She laughed. "I realize that the Forester is the same as the one in my . . . when I visited here so long ago, but he certainly didn't recognize me."

"No doubt of that," Wisp said with a grin playing at the edges of his wide mouth.

"I wonder what he is thrashing about in the forest to find. He hasn't had much luck."

"No, he hasn't, has he?" And Wisp chuckled

58

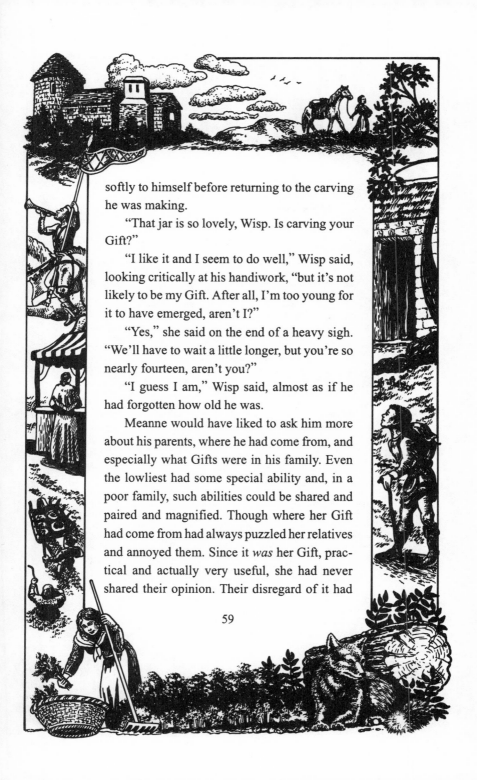

softly to himself before returning to the carving he was making.

"That jar is so lovely, Wisp. Is carving your Gift?"

"I like it and I seem to do well," Wisp said, looking critically at his handiwork, "but it's not likely to be my Gift. After all, I'm too young for it to have emerged, aren't I?"

"Yes," she said on the end of a heavy sigh. "We'll have to wait a little longer, but you're so nearly fourteen, aren't you?"

"I guess I am," Wisp said, almost as if he had forgotten how old he was.

Meanne would have liked to ask him more about his parents, where he had come from, and especially what Gifts were in his family. Even the lowliest had some special ability and, in a poor family, such abilities could be shared and paired and magnified. Though where her Gift had come from had always puzzled her relatives and annoyed them. Since it *was* her Gift, practical and actually very useful, she had never shared their opinion. Their disregard of it had

59

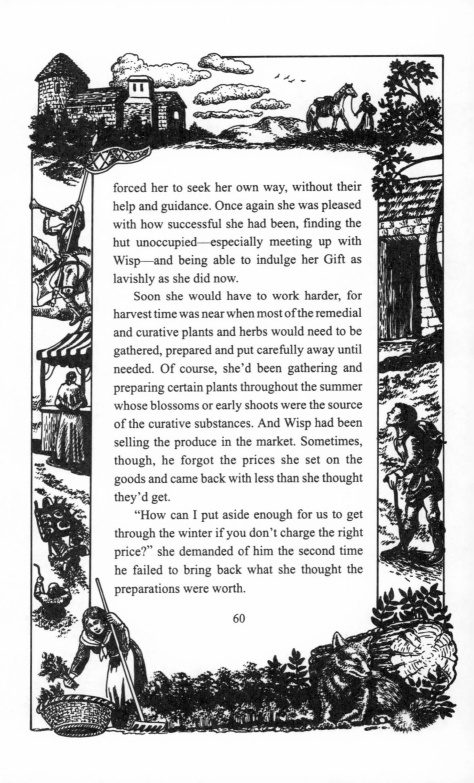

forced her to seek her own way, without their help and guidance. Once again she was pleased with how successful she had been, finding the hut unoccupied—especially meeting up with Wisp—and being able to indulge her Gift as lavishly as she did now.

Soon she would have to work harder, for harvest time was near when most of the remedial and curative plants and herbs would need to be gathered, prepared and put carefully away until needed. Of course, she'd been gathering and preparing certain plants throughout the summer whose blossoms or early shoots were the source of the curative substances. And Wisp had been selling the produce in the market. Sometimes, though, he forgot the prices she set on the goods and came back with less than she thought they'd get.

"How can I put aside enough for us to get through the winter if you don't charge the right price?" she demanded of him the second time he failed to bring back what she thought the preparations were worth.

60

"Come yourself, then, and see that the right price is paid," he'd replied without a trace of remorse.

"You know I can't."

"Why not?" and he turned very wide blue eyes at her in surprise. "You'd be safe enough with me!"

"Safe?"

"Forester never harmed you, did he?" Then Wisp leaned toward her. "You know what? You're getting woodsy."

"Woodsy?" Even to her own ears her exclamation sounded shrill and strident. "Woodsy?" she repeated with less heat and more scorn.

"My mum said she was always the better for having a chance to chat with other wives and mothers."

"I'm neither wife nor mother . . . and stop grinning like that. *You* were the one who cast me in that role!"

"Me ol' mum," and he imitated the voice she had used. "Tell you what . . . if I fix you up, no one'll ever guess that a pretty lady lives behind

61

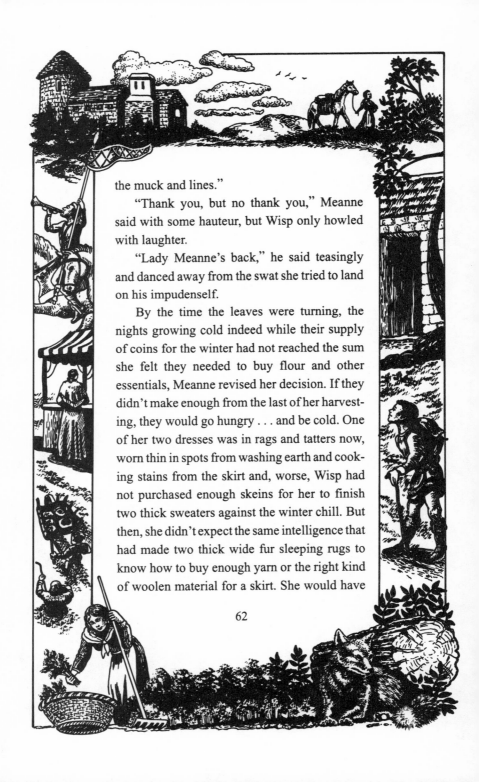

the muck and lines."

"Thank you, but no thank you," Meanne said with some hauteur, but Wisp only howled with laughter.

"Lady Meanne's back," he said teasingly and danced away from the swat she tried to land on his impudenself.

By the time the leaves were turning, the nights growing cold indeed while their supply of coins for the winter had not reached the sum she felt they needed to buy flour and other essentials, Meanne revised her decision. If they didn't make enough from the last of her harvesting, they would go hungry . . . and be cold. One of her two dresses was in rags and tatters now, worn thin in spots from washing earth and cooking stains from the skirt and, worse, Wisp had not purchased enough skeins for her to finish two thick sweaters against the winter chill. But then, she didn't expect the same intelligence that had made two thick wide fur sleeping rugs to know how to buy enough yarn or the right kind of woolen material for a skirt. She would have

62

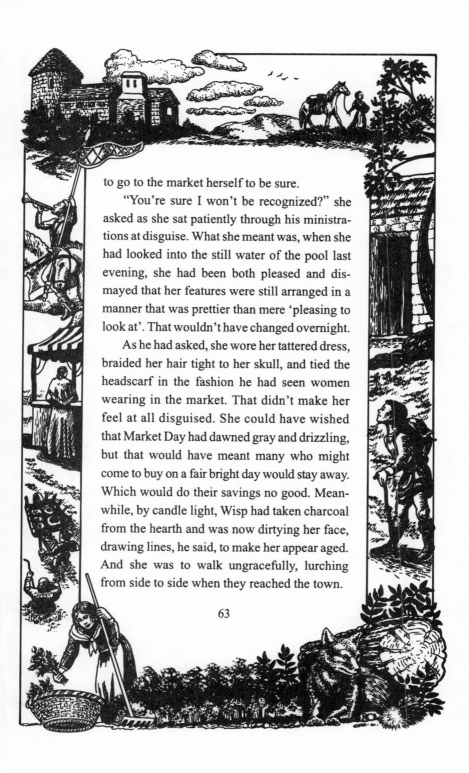

to go to the market herself to be sure.

"You're sure I won't be recognized?" she asked as she sat patiently through his ministrations at disguise. What she meant was, when she had looked into the still water of the pool last evening, she had been both pleased and dismayed that her features were still arranged in a manner that was prettier than mere 'pleasing to look at'. That wouldn't have changed overnight.

As he had asked, she wore her tattered dress, braided her hair tight to her skull, and tied the headscarf in the fashion he had seen women wearing in the market. That didn't make her feel at all disguised. She could have wished that Market Day had dawned gray and drizzling, but that would have meant many who might come to buy on a fair bright day would stay away. Which would do their savings no good. Meanwhile, by candle light, Wisp had taken charcoal from the hearth and was now dirtying her face, drawing lines, he said, to make her appear aged. And she was to walk ungracefully, lurching from side to side when they reached the town.

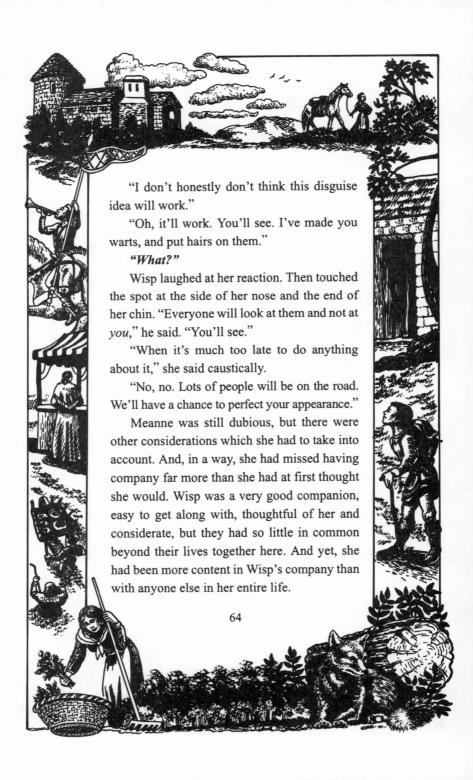

"I don't honestly don't think this disguise idea will work."

"Oh, it'll work. You'll see. I've made you warts, and put hairs on them."

"What?"

Wisp laughed at her reaction. Then touched the spot at the side of her nose and the end of her chin. "Everyone will look at them and not at *you*," he said. "You'll see."

"When it's much too late to do anything about it," she said caustically.

"No, no. Lots of people will be on the road. We'll have a chance to perfect your appearance."

Meanne was still dubious, but there were other considerations which she had to take into account. And, in a way, she had missed having company far more than she had at first thought she would. Wisp was a very good companion, easy to get along with, thoughtful of her and considerate, but they had so little in common beyond their lives together here. And yet, she had been more content in Wisp's company than with anyone else in her entire life.

64

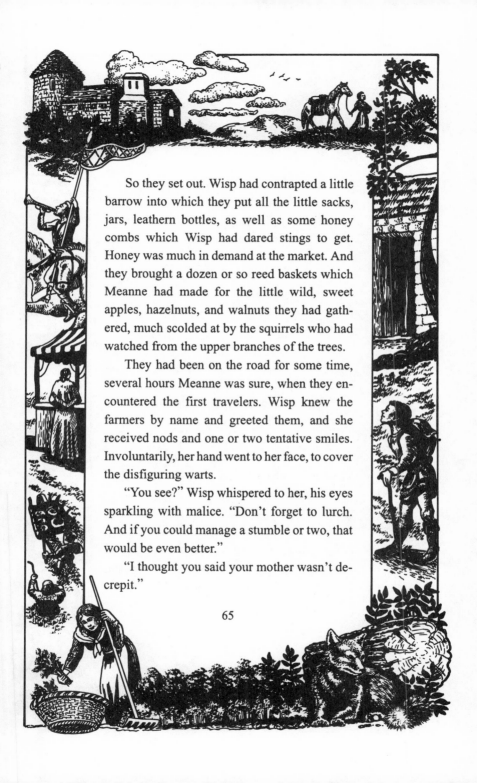

So they set out. Wisp had contrapted a little barrow into which they put all the little sacks, jars, leathern bottles, as well as some honey combs which Wisp had dared stings to get. Honey was much in demand at the market. And they brought a dozen or so reed baskets which Meanne had made for the little wild, sweet apples, hazelnuts, and walnuts they had gathered, much scolded at by the squirrels who had watched from the upper branches of the trees.

They had been on the road for some time, several hours Meanne was sure, when they encountered the first travelers. Wisp knew the farmers by name and greeted them, and she received nods and one or two tentative smiles. Involuntarily, her hand went to her face, to cover the disfiguring warts.

"You see?" Wisp whispered to her, his eyes sparkling with malice. "Don't forget to lurch. And if you could manage a stumble or two, that would be even better."

"I thought you said your mother wasn't decrepit."

65

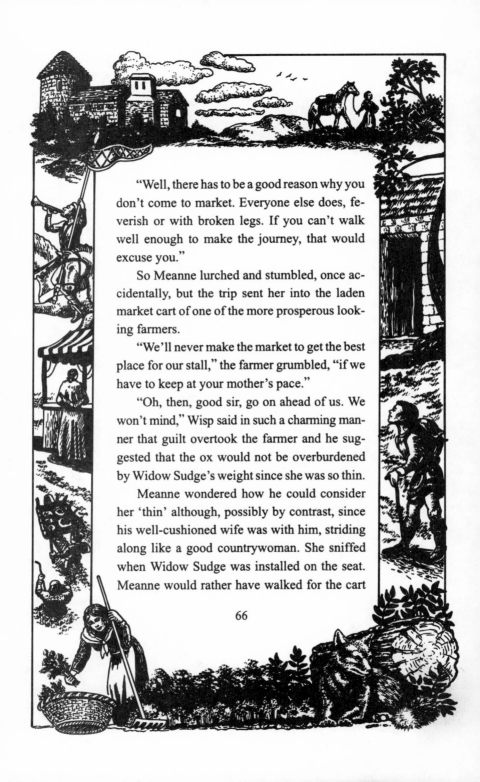

"Well, there has to be a good reason why you don't come to market. Everyone else does, feverish or with broken legs. If you can't walk well enough to make the journey, that would excuse you."

So Meanne lurched and stumbled, once accidentally, but the trip sent her into the laden market cart of one of the more prosperous looking farmers.

"We'll never make the market to get the best place for our stall," the farmer grumbled, "if we have to keep at your mother's pace."

"Oh, then, good sir, go on ahead of us. We won't mind," Wisp said in such a charming manner that guilt overtook the farmer and he suggested that the ox would not be overburdened by Widow Sudge's weight since she was so thin.

Meanne wondered how he could consider her 'thin' although, possibly by contrast, since his well-cushioned wife was with him, striding along like a good countrywoman. She sniffed when Widow Sudge was installed on the seat. Meanne would rather have walked for the cart

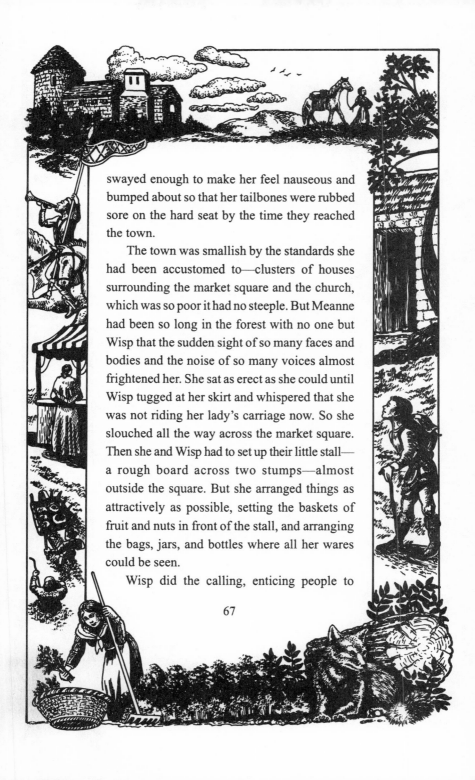

swayed enough to make her feel nauseous and
bumped about so that her tailbones were rubbed
sore on the hard seat by the time they reached
the town.

The town was smallish by the standards she
had been accustomed to—clusters of houses
surrounding the market square and the church,
which was so poor it had no steeple. But Meanne
had been so long in the forest with no one but
Wisp that the sudden sight of so many faces and
bodies and the noise of so many voices almost
frightened her. She sat as erect as she could until
Wisp tugged at her skirt and whispered that she
was not riding her lady's carriage now. So she
slouched all the way across the market square.
Then she and Wisp had to set up their little stall—
a rough board across two stumps—almost
outside the square. But she arranged things as
attractively as possible, setting the baskets of
fruit and nuts in front of the stall, and arranging
the bags, jars, and bottles where all her wares
could be seen.

Wisp did the calling, enticing people to

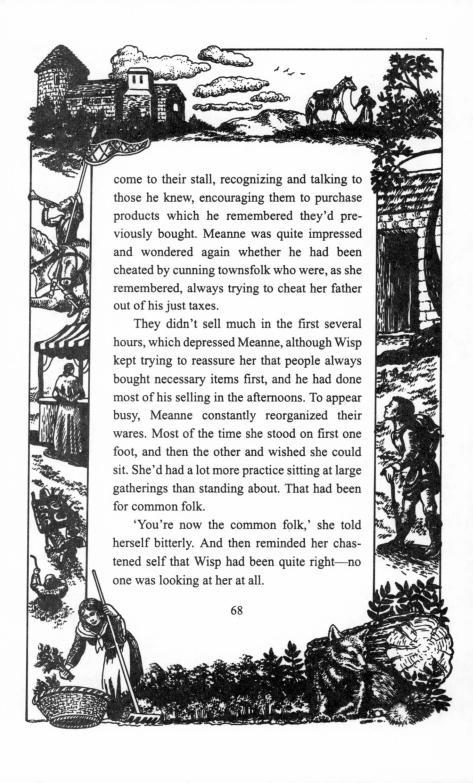

come to their stall, recognizing and talking to those he knew, encouraging them to purchase products which he remembered they'd previously bought. Meanne was quite impressed and wondered again whether he had been cheated by cunning townsfolk who were, as she remembered, always trying to cheat her father out of his just taxes.

They didn't sell much in the first several hours, which depressed Meanne, although Wisp kept trying to reassure her that people always bought necessary items first, and he had done most of his selling in the afternoons. To appear busy, Meanne constantly reorganized their wares. Most of the time she stood on first one foot, and then the other and wished she could sit. She'd had a lot more practice sitting at large gatherings than standing about. That had been for common folk.

'You're now the common folk,' she told herself bitterly. And then reminded her chastened self that Wisp had been quite right—no one was looking at her at all.

68

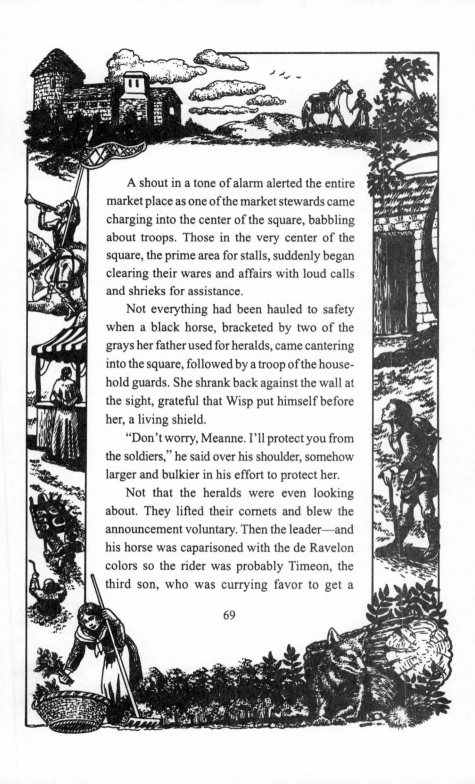

A shout in a tone of alarm alerted the entire market place as one of the market stewards came charging into the center of the square, babbling about troops. Those in the very center of the square, the prime area for stalls, suddenly began clearing their wares and affairs with loud calls and shrieks for assistance.

Not everything had been hauled to safety when a black horse, bracketed by two of the grays her father used for heralds, came cantering into the square, followed by a troop of the house-hold guards. She shrank back against the wall at the sight, grateful that Wisp put himself before her, a living shield.

"Don't worry, Meanne. I'll protect you from the soldiers," he said over his shoulder, somehow larger and bulkier in his effort to protect her.

Not that the heralds were even looking about. They lifted their cornets and blew the announcement voluntary. Then the leader—and his horse was caparisoned with the de Ravelon colors so the rider was probably Timeon, the third son, who was currying favor to get a

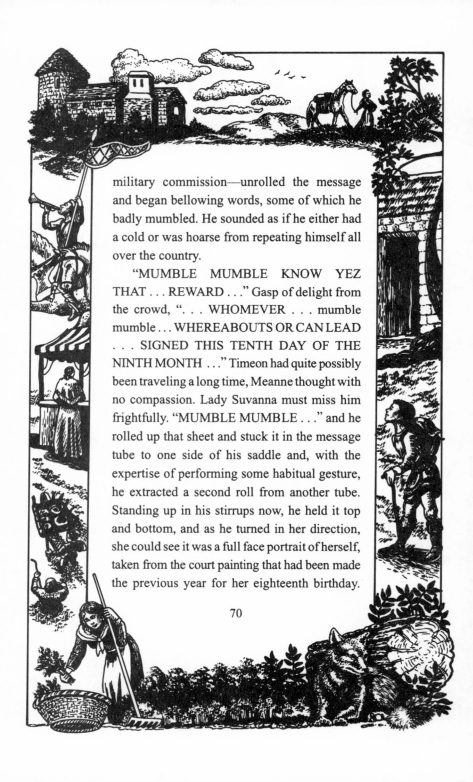

military commission—unrolled the message and began bellowing words, some of which he badly mumbled. He sounded as if he either had a cold or was hoarse from repeating himself all over the country.

"MUMBLE MUMBLE KNOW YEZ THAT . . . REWARD . . ." Gasp of delight from the crowd, ". . . WHOMEVER . . . mumble mumble . . . WHEREABOUTS OR CAN LEAD . . . SIGNED THIS TENTH DAY OF THE NINTH MONTH . . ." Timeon had quite possibly been traveling a long time, Meanne thought with no compassion. Lady Suvanna must miss him frightfully. "MUMBLE MUMBLE . . ." and he rolled up that sheet and stuck it in the message tube to one side of his saddle and, with the expertise of performing some habitual gesture, he extracted a second roll from another tube. Standing up in his stirrups now, he held it top and bottom, and as he turned in her direction, she could see it was a full face portrait of herself, taken from the court painting that had been made the previous year for her eighteenth birthday.

70

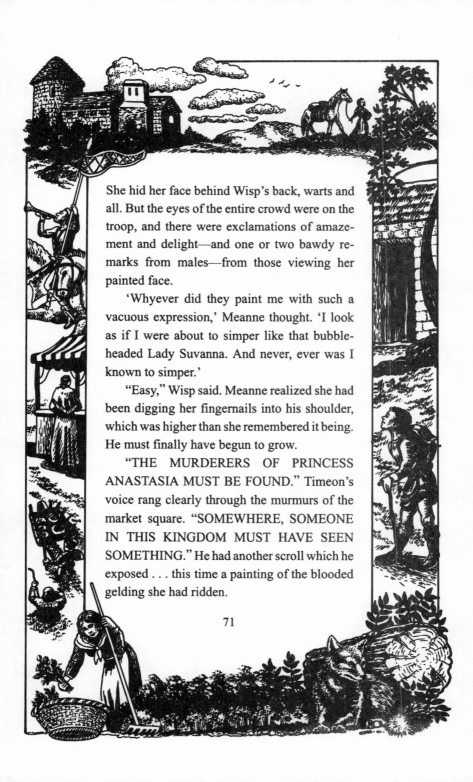

She hid her face behind Wisp's back, warts and all. But the eyes of the entire crowd were on the troop, and there were exclamations of amazement and delight—and one or two bawdy remarks from males—from those viewing her painted face.

'Whyever did they paint me with such a vacuous expression,' Meanne thought. 'I look as if I were about to simper like that bubble-headed Lady Suvanna. And never, ever was I known to simper.'

"Easy," Wisp said. Meanne realized she had been digging her fingernails into his shoulder, which was higher than she remembered it being. He must finally have begun to grow.

"THE MURDERERS OF PRINCESS ANASTASIA MUST BE FOUND." Timeon's voice rang clearly through the murmurs of the market square. "SOMEWHERE, SOMEONE IN THIS KINGDOM MUST HAVE SEEN SOMETHING." He had another scroll which he exposed . . . this time a painting of the blooded gelding she had ridden.

71

Good heavens, she had staged her death rather too authentically. That was both a relief—because it meant they were not looking for a *live* person—and dismay, that she was being mourned. She really hadn't meant to cause everyone grief . . . even her father for wanting to marry her off to that dreadful Baron.

Still, as no one could have seen her or her erstwhile murderer, Timeon's quest was doomed to failure. That is, unless he came close enough to identify her. He was dismounting now, and so were the heralds and troops. Small boys had been enticed from the crowd as horse holders, and the liveried men were moving around, each of them carrying a smaller replica of that awful court portrait and showing it to everyone.

"Don't *worry*," Wisp said to her. "They won't recognize you from that picture, I assure you."

"Yes, but Timeon knows me."

"He does, Princess?" Wisp said in a low voice, his eyes dancing with a dark and suddenly menacing light.

Would Wisp turn her in? For the reward? It

72

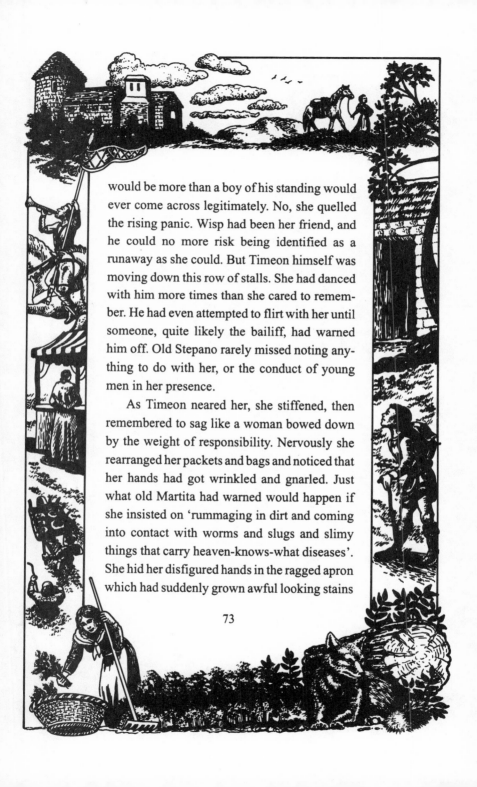

would be more than a boy of his standing would ever come across legitimately. No, she quelled the rising panic. Wisp had been her friend, and he could no more risk being identified as a runaway as she could. But Timeon himself was moving down this row of stalls. She had danced with him more times than she cared to remember. He had even attempted to flirt with her until someone, quite likely the bailiff, had warned him off. Old Stepano rarely missed noting anything to do with her, or the conduct of young men in her presence.

As Timeon neared her, she stiffened, then remembered to sag like a woman bowed down by the weight of responsibility. Nervously she rearranged her packets and bags and noticed that her hands had got wrinkled and gnarled. Just what old Martita had warned would happen if she insisted on 'rummaging in dirt and coming into contact with worms and slugs and slimy things that carry heaven-knows-what diseases'. She hid her disfigured hands in the ragged apron which had suddenly grown awful looking stains

73

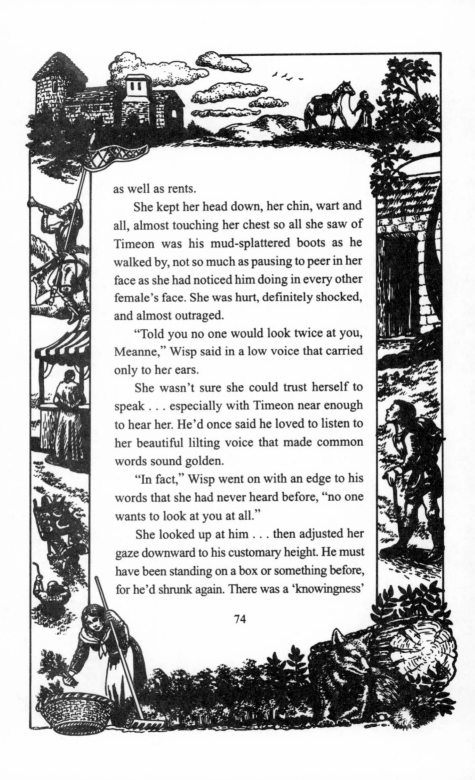

as well as rents.

She kept her head down, her chin, wart and all, almost touching her chest so all she saw of Timeon was his mud-splattered boots as he walked by, not so much as pausing to peer in her face as she had noticed him doing in every other female's face. She was hurt, definitely shocked, and almost outraged.

"Told you no one would look twice at you, Meanne," Wisp said in a low voice that carried only to her ears.

She wasn't sure she could trust herself to speak . . . especially with Timeon near enough to hear her. He'd once said he loved to listen to her beautiful lilting voice that made common words sound golden.

"In fact," Wisp went on with an edge to his words that she had never heard before, "no one wants to look at you at all."

She looked up at him . . . then adjusted her gaze downward to his customary height. He must have been standing on a box or something before, for he'd shrunk again. There was a 'knowingness'

74

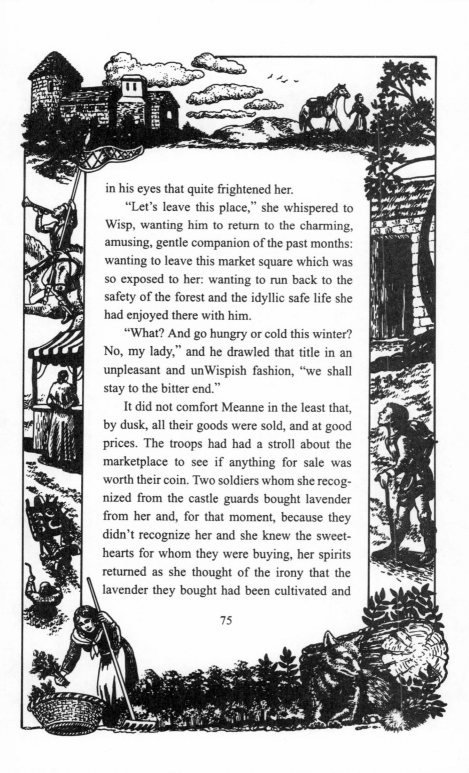

in his eyes that quite frightened her.

"Let's leave this place," she whispered to Wisp, wanting him to return to the charming, amusing, gentle companion of the past months: wanting to leave this market square which was so exposed to her: wanting to run back to the safety of the forest and the idyllic safe life she had enjoyed there with him.

"What? And go hungry or cold this winter? No, my lady," and he drawled that title in an unpleasant and unWispish fashion, "we shall stay to the bitter end."

It did not comfort Meanne in the least that, by dusk, all their goods were sold, and at good prices. The troops had had a stroll about the marketplace to see if anything for sale was worth their coin. Two soldiers whom she recognized from the castle guards bought lavender from her and, for that moment, because they didn't recognize her and she knew the sweethearts for whom they were buying, her spirits returned as she thought of the irony that the lavender they bought had been cultivated and

75

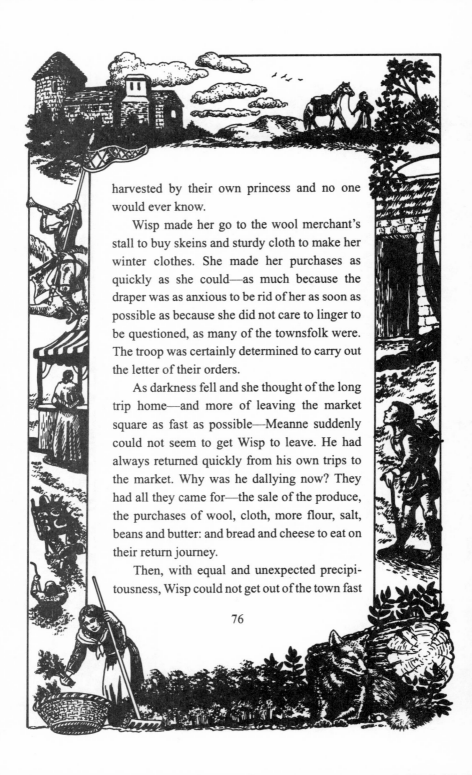

harvested by their own princess and no one would ever know.

Wisp made her go to the wool merchant's stall to buy skeins and sturdy cloth to make her winter clothes. She made her purchases as quickly as she could—as much because the draper was as anxious to be rid of her as soon as possible as because she did not care to linger to be questioned, as many of the townsfolk were. The troop was certainly determined to carry out the letter of their orders.

As darkness fell and she thought of the long trip home—and more of leaving the market square as fast as possible—Meanne suddenly could not seem to get Wisp to leave. He had always returned quickly from his own trips to the market. Why was he dallying now? They had all they came for—the sale of the produce, the purchases of wool, cloth, more flour, salt, beans and butter: and bread and cheese to eat on their return journey.

Then, with equal and unexpected precipitousness, Wisp could not get out of the town fast

76

enough. He even set her in the barrow—"you're not supposed to walk fast, you know"—and was pushing her through the gates before she knew what was what.

"And why the haste, Master Wisp?" she asked, annoyance and indignity making her waspish.

"The troops are now asking who's new in this area and I do not want them looking me over."

"But you surely don't think *you'd* be suspected of murdering me?" She was so amused at such conceit that she laughed, and he deliberately pushed the barrow into a pothole, making her teeth rattle. When she tried to climb out, a very hard strong hand on her shoulder thwarted the action.

"I may yet, madame," he said, once more in that hard tone of voice that was so unWispish.

A little more frightened by this change in Wisp than she ever thought she could be, she subsided until they were well past the first of the farms. She could hear the lowing of unmilked

77

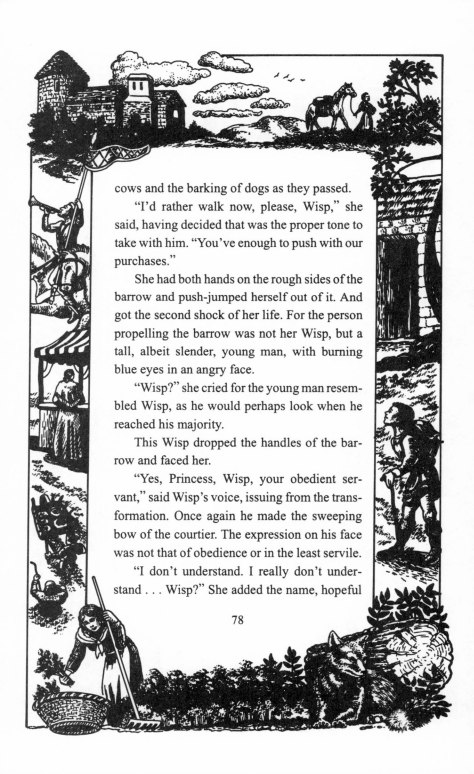

cows and the barking of dogs as they passed.

"I'd rather walk now, please, Wisp," she said, having decided that was the proper tone to take with him. "You've enough to push with our purchases."

She had both hands on the rough sides of the barrow and push-jumped herself out of it. And got the second shock of her life. For the person propelling the barrow was not her Wisp, but a tall, albeit slender, young man, with burning blue eyes in an angry face.

"Wisp?" she cried for the young man resembled Wisp, as he would perhaps look when he reached his majority.

This Wisp dropped the handles of the barrow and faced her.

"Yes, Princess, Wisp, your obedient servant," said Wisp's voice, issuing from the transformation. Once again he made the sweeping bow of the courtier. The expression on his face was not that of obedience or in the least servile.

"I don't understand. I really don't understand . . . Wisp?" She added the name, hopeful

78

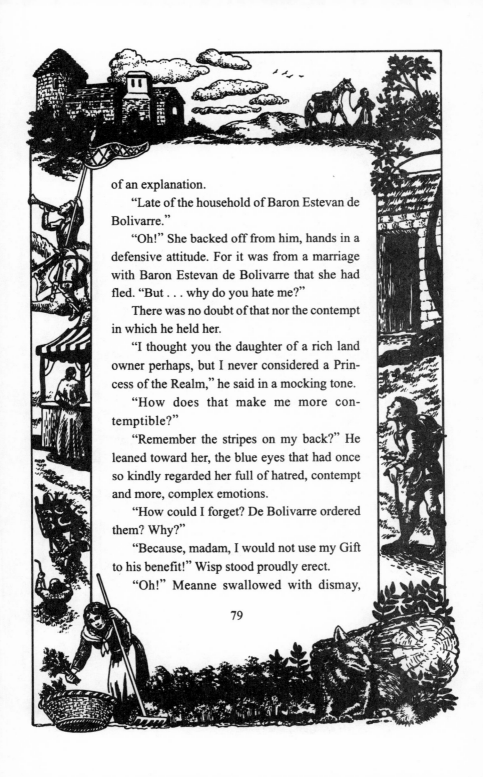

of an explanation.

"Late of the household of Baron Estevan de Bolivarre."

"Oh!" She backed off from him, hands in a defensive attitude. For it was from a marriage with Baron Estevan de Bolivarre that she had fled. "But . . . why do you hate me?"

There was no doubt of that nor the contempt in which he held her.

"I thought you the daughter of a rich land owner perhaps, but I never considered a Princess of the Realm," he said in a mocking tone.

"How does that make me more contemptible?"

"Remember the stripes on my back?" He leaned toward her, the blue eyes that had once so kindly regarded her full of hatred, contempt and more, complex emotions.

"How could I forget? De Bolivarre ordered them? Why?"

"Because, madam, I would not use my Gift to his benefit!" Wisp stood proudly erect.

"Oh!" Meanne swallowed with dismay,

79

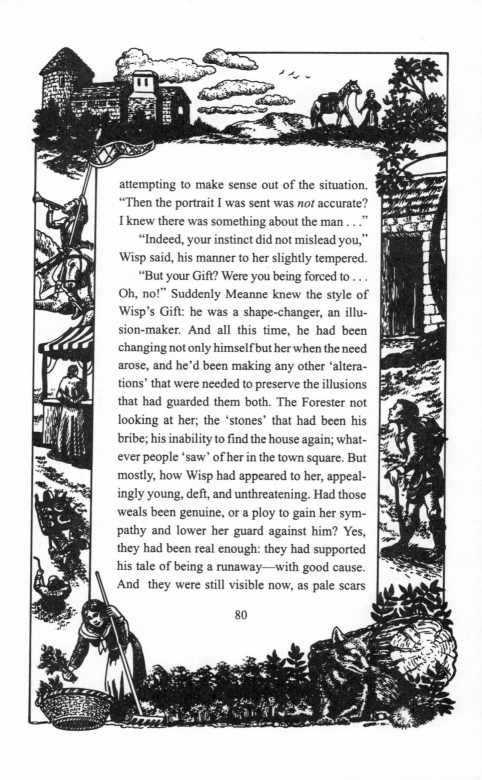

attempting to make sense out of the situation. "Then the portrait I was sent was *not* accurate? I knew there was something about the man . . ."

"Indeed, your instinct did not mislead you," Wisp said, his manner to her slightly tempered.

"But your Gift? Were you being forced to . . . Oh, no!" Suddenly Meanne knew the style of Wisp's Gift: he was a shape-changer, an illusion-maker. And all this time, he had been changing not only himself but her when the need arose, and he'd been making any other 'alterations' that were needed to preserve the illusions that had guarded them both. The Forester not looking at her; the 'stones' that had been his bribe; his inability to find the house again; whatever people 'saw' of her in the town square. But mostly, how Wisp had appeared to her, appealingly young, deft, and unthreatening. Had those weals been genuine, or a ploy to gain her sympathy and lower her guard against him? Yes, they had been real enough: they had supported his tale of being a runaway—with good cause. And they were still visible now, as pale scars

80

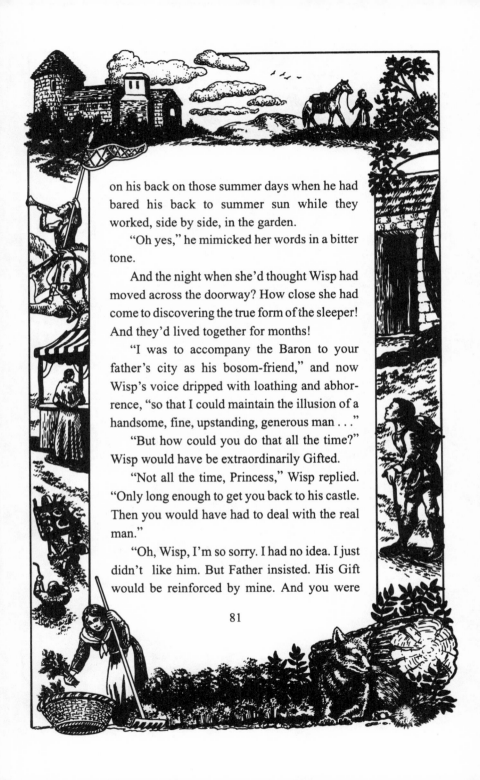

on his back on those summer days when he had bared his back to summer sun while they worked, side by side, in the garden.

"Oh yes," he mimicked her words in a bitter tone.

And the night when she'd thought Wisp had moved across the doorway? How close she had come to discovering the true form of the sleeper! And they'd lived together for months!

"I was to accompany the Baron to your father's city as his bosom-friend," and now Wisp's voice dripped with loathing and abhorrence, "so that I could maintain the illusion of a handsome, fine, upstanding, generous man . . ."

"But how could you do that all the time?" Wisp would have be extraordinarily Gifted.

"Not all the time, Princess," Wisp replied. "Only long enough to get you back to his castle. Then you would have had to deal with the real man."

"Oh, Wisp, I'm so sorry. I had no idea. I just didn't like him. But Father insisted. His Gift would be reinforced by mine. And you were

81

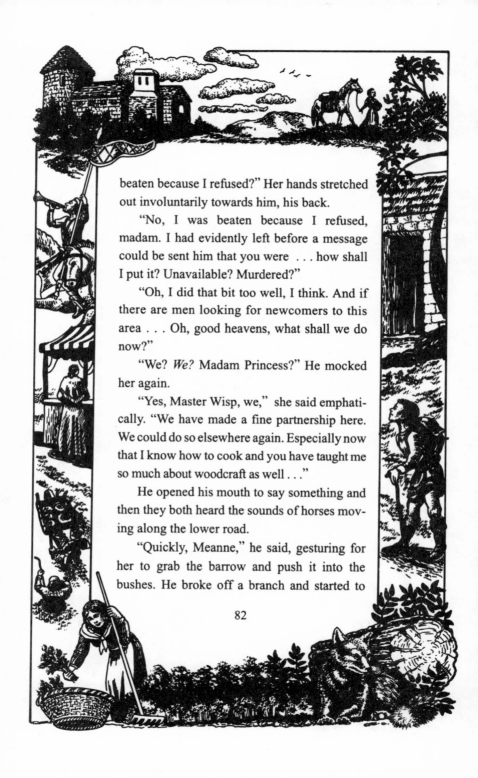

beaten because I refused?" Her hands stretched out involuntarily towards him, his back.

"No, I was beaten because I refused, madam. I had evidently left before a message could be sent him that you were . . . how shall I put it? Unavailable? Murdered?"

"Oh, I did that bit too well, I think. And if there are men looking for newcomers to this area . . . Oh, good heavens, what shall we do now?"

"We? *We?* Madam Princess?" He mocked her again.

"Yes, Master Wisp, we," she said emphatically. "We have made a fine partnership here. We could do so elsewhere again. Especially now that I know how to cook and you have taught me so much about woodcraft as well . . ."

He opened his mouth to say something and then they both heard the sounds of horses moving along the lower road.

"Quickly, Meanne," he said, gesturing for her to grab the barrow and push it into the bushes. He broke off a branch and started to

82

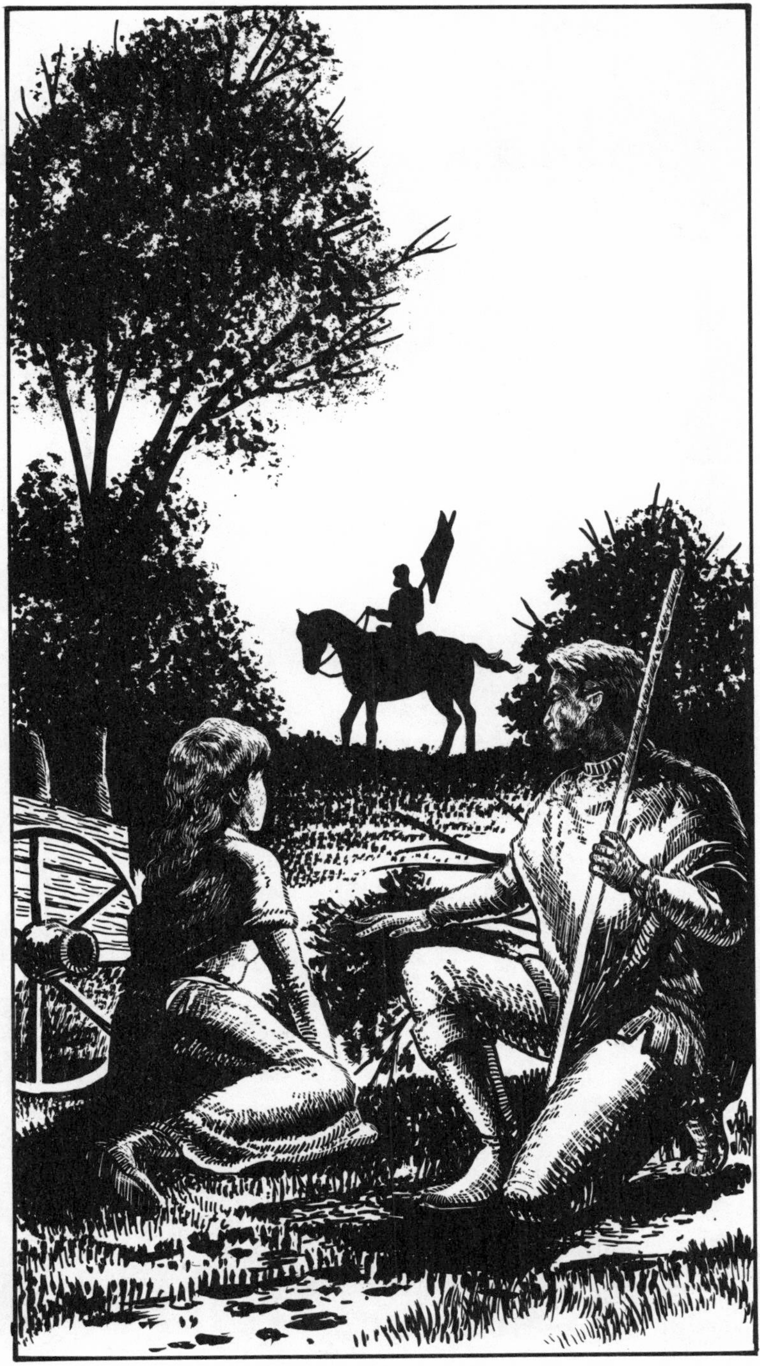

erase the tell-tale barrow wheel mark as far back
as the last lane.

"Just in case," he said when he joined her in
the dense undergrowth.

The troop, however, rode by, bridles jin-
gling, the men murmuring among themselves as
they trotted past.

"Do you think they're heading for our
home?" Meanne asked in a whisper as if her soft
voice might alert their pursuers.

"That's possible, though that road leads
elsewhere, too. And who," now he turned his
gaze on her again and she was breathlessly
relieved to see some softening in his manner
toward her, "would think the Princess Anastasia
found shelter in a ruined hut?"

"Being born a princess often has little to do
with one's private goals in life," she said rather
caustically. "I was ridiculed, tormented, teased,
chastised, and physically prevented from using
my Gift because it was so," and she altered her
tone to rounded vowels and haughty consonants,
"'unsuitable for a princess of the Blood Royal to

84

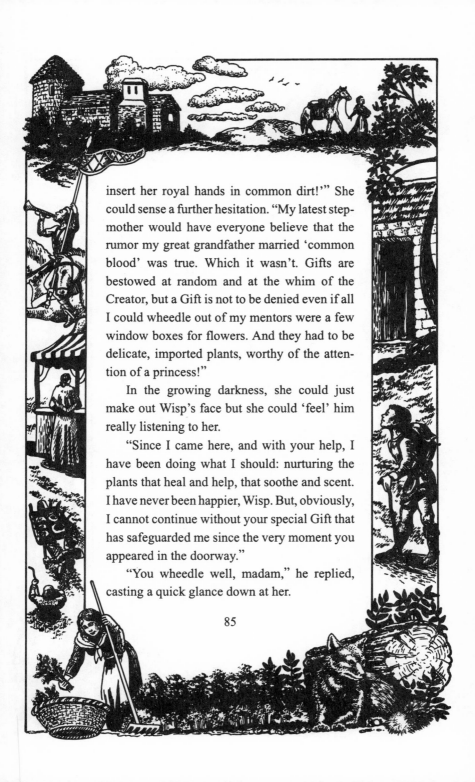

insert her royal hands in common dirt!'" She could sense a further hesitation. "My latest stepmother would have everyone believe that the rumor my great grandfather married 'common blood' was true. Which it wasn't. Gifts are bestowed at random and at the whim of the Creator, but a Gift is not to be denied even if all I could wheedle out of my mentors were a few window boxes for flowers. And they had to be delicate, imported plants, worthy of the attention of a princess!"

In the growing darkness, she could just make out Wisp's face but she could 'feel' him really listening to her.

"Since I came here, and with your help, I have been doing what I should: nurturing the plants that heal and help, that soothe and scent. I have never been happier, Wisp. But, obviously, I cannot continue without your special Gift that has safeguarded me since the very moment you appeared in the doorway."

"You wheedle well, madam," he replied, casting a quick glance down at her.

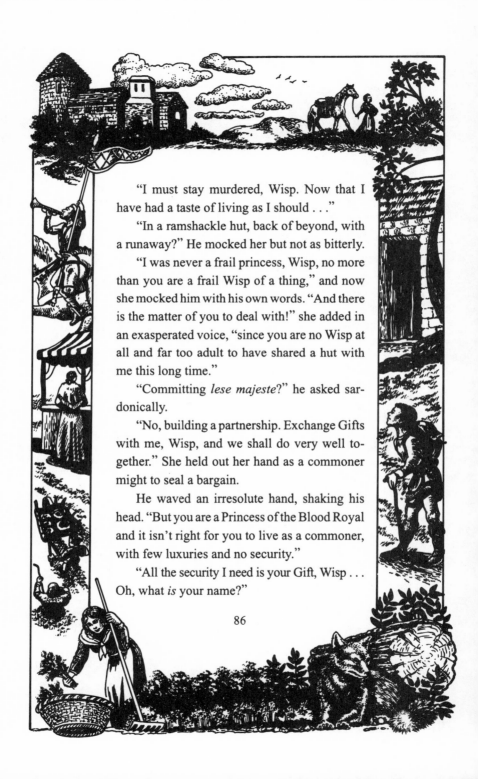

"I must stay murdered, Wisp. Now that I have had a taste of living as I should . . ."

"In a ramshackle hut, back of beyond, with a runaway?" He mocked her but not as bitterly.

"I was never a frail princess, Wisp, no more than you are a frail Wisp of a thing," and now she mocked him with his own words. "And there is the matter of you to deal with!" she added in an exasperated voice, "since you are no Wisp at all and far too adult to have shared a hut with me this long time."

"Committing *lese majeste*?" he asked sardonically.

"No, building a partnership. Exchange Gifts with me, Wisp, and we shall do very well together." She held out her hand as a commoner might to seal a bargain.

He waved an irresolute hand, shaking his head. "But you are a Princess of the Blood Royal and it isn't right for you to live as a commoner, with few luxuries and no security."

"All the security I need is your Gift, Wisp . . . Oh, what *is* your name?"

86

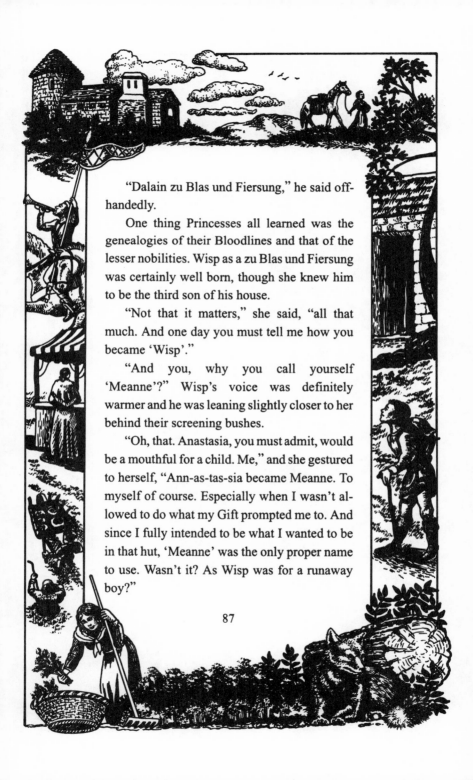

"Dalain zu Blas und Fiersung," he said off-handedly.

One thing Princesses all learned was the genealogies of their Bloodlines and that of the lesser nobilities. Wisp as a zu Blas und Fiersung was certainly well born, though she knew him to be the third son of his house.

"Not that it matters," she said, "all that much. And one day you must tell me how you became 'Wisp'."

"And you, why you call yourself 'Meanne'?" Wisp's voice was definitely warmer and he was leaning slightly closer to her behind their screening bushes.

"Oh, that. Anastasia, you must admit, would be a mouthful for a child. Me," and she gestured to herself, "Ann-as-tas-sia became Meanne. To myself of course. Especially when I wasn't allowed to do what my Gift prompted me to. And since I fully intended to be what I wanted to be in that hut, 'Meanne' was the only proper name to use. Wasn't it? As Wisp was for a runaway boy?"

87

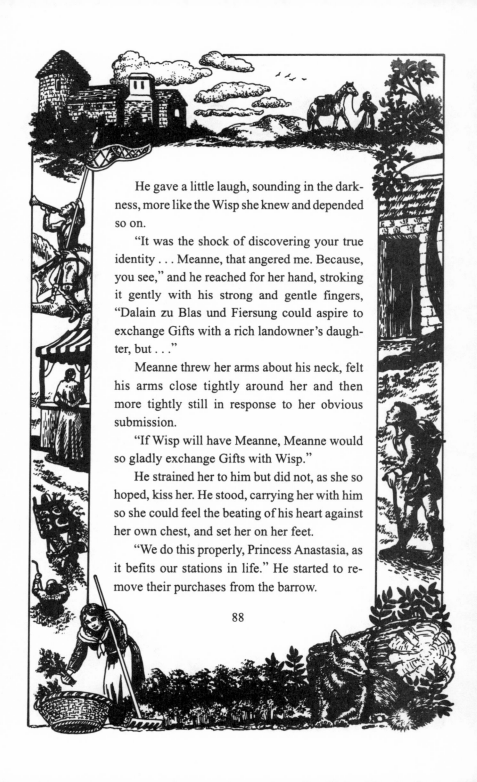

He gave a little laugh, sounding in the darkness, more like the Wisp she knew and depended so on.

"It was the shock of discovering your true identity . . . Meanne, that angered me. Because, you see," and he reached for her hand, stroking it gently with his strong and gentle fingers, "Dalain zu Blas und Fiersung could aspire to exchange Gifts with a rich landowner's daughter, but . . ."

Meanne threw her arms about his neck, felt his arms close tightly around her and then more tightly still in response to her obvious submission.

"If Wisp will have Meanne, Meanne would so gladly exchange Gifts with Wisp."

He strained her to him but did not, as she so hoped, kiss her. He stood, carrying her with him so she could feel the beating of his heart against her own chest, and set her on her feet.

"We do this properly, Princess Anastasia, as it befits our stations in life." He started to remove their purchases from the barrow.

88

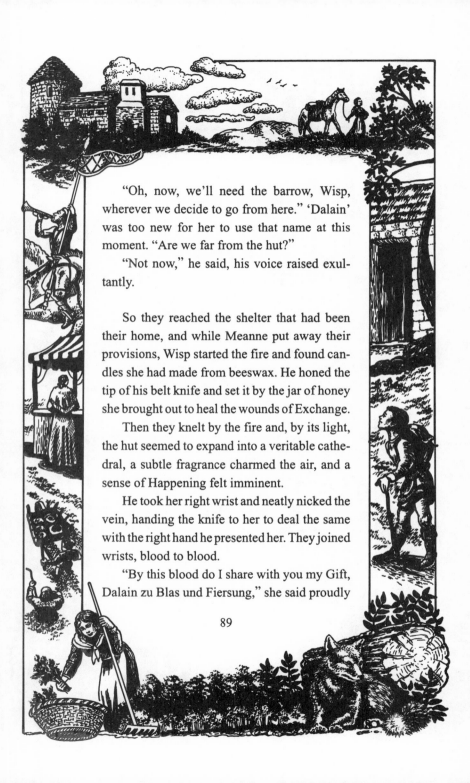

"Oh, now, we'll need the barrow, Wisp, wherever we decide to go from here." 'Dalain' was too new for her to use that name at this moment. "Are we far from the hut?"

"Not now," he said, his voice raised exultantly.

So they reached the shelter that had been their home, and while Meanne put away their provisions, Wisp started the fire and found candles she had made from beeswax. He honed the tip of his belt knife and set it by the jar of honey she brought out to heal the wounds of Exchange.

Then they knelt by the fire and, by its light, the hut seemed to expand into a veritable cathedral, a subtle fragrance charmed the air, and a sense of Happening felt imminent.

He took her right wrist and neatly nicked the vein, handing the knife to her to deal the same with the right hand he presented her. They joined wrists, blood to blood.

"By this blood do I share with you my Gift, Dalain zu Blas und Fiersung," she said proudly

89

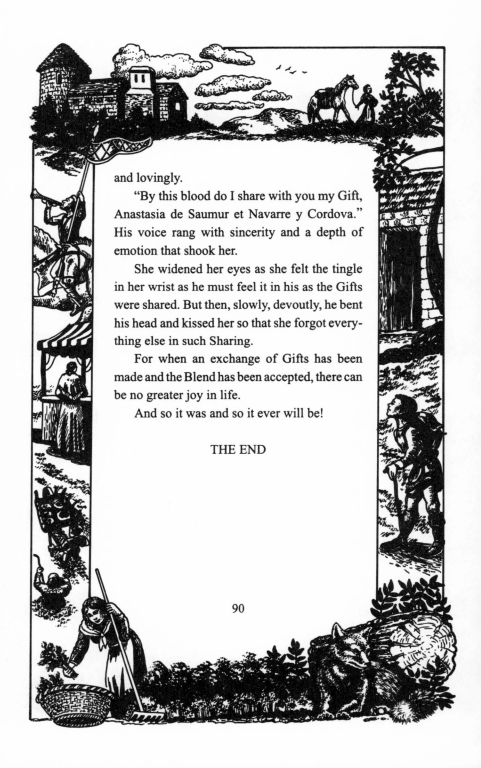

and lovingly.

"By this blood do I share with you my Gift, Anastasia de Saumur et Navarre y Cordova." His voice rang with sincerity and a depth of emotion that shook her.

She widened her eyes as she felt the tingle in her wrist as he must feel it in his as the Gifts were shared. But then, slowly, devoutly, he bent his head and kissed her so that she forgot everything else in such Sharing.

For when an exchange of Gifts has been made and the Blend has been accepted, there can be no greater joy in life.

And so it was and so it ever will be!

THE END

90

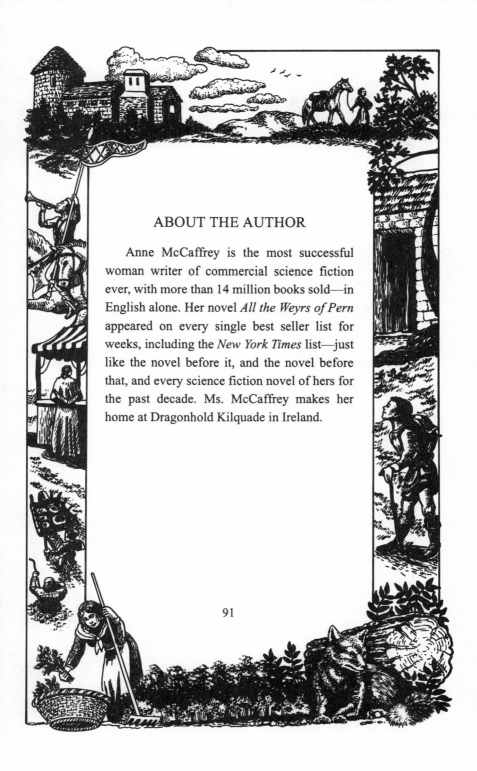

ABOUT THE AUTHOR

Anne McCaffrey is the most successful woman writer of commercial science fiction ever, with more than 14 million books sold—in English alone. Her novel *All the Weyrs of Pern* appeared on every single best seller list for weeks, including the *New York Times* list—just like the novel before it, and the novel before that, and every science fiction novel of hers for the past decade. Ms. McCaffrey makes her home at Dragonhold Kilquade in Ireland.

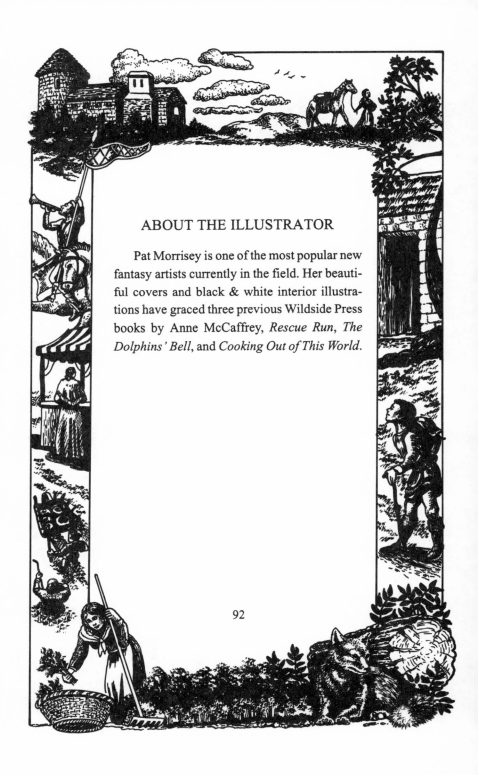

ABOUT THE ILLUSTRATOR

Pat Morrisey is one of the most popular new fantasy artists currently in the field. Her beautiful covers and black & white interior illustrations have graced three previous Wildside Press books by Anne McCaffrey, *Rescue Run*, *The Dolphins' Bell*, and *Cooking Out of This World*.

92